Witchcraft in the Church

Witchcraft in the Church

Hélèné Fulton

Light the World Ministries
2014

Copyright © 2014 by Hélèné Fulton

All rights reserved. This book or any portion thereof may not be reproduced or used in any manner whatsoever without the express written permission of the publisher.

First Printing: 2014

ISBN 978-0-620-59396-0

Light the World Ministries

www.lighttheworldministries.co.za

For any help or orders e-mail our office:
churchoffice@lighttheworldministries.co.za

Ordering Information:
Special discounts are available on quantity purchases by corporations, associations, educators, and others. For details, contact the publisher at the above listed e-mail address.

U.S. trade bookstores and wholesalers:

Please contact Light the World Ministries on e-mail address below.
churchoffice@lighttheworldministries.co.za

Dedication

For all the unconditional love, guidance and teachings, all glory to:

God the Father
God the Son
God the Holy Spirit

To my loving husband Robert thank you. Without your support, and love, I would have never completed this book.

To Michael Bradley – Thank you for being a Spirit filled teacher

A special thanks to all my spiritual children for your support.

Tanja Davey – Thank you for allowing the Holy Spirit to guide you in the design of the cover for this book.

Leeanne Naicker last but certainly not least – Thank you for all the help with the editing of this book.

Contents

Foreword viii

Preface xi

Introduction 1

Chapter 1: Visions & Dreams 7

Chapter 2: Who is the Church? 21

Chapter 3: Hurt by the Church 31

Chapter 4: The Fish Eagle 39

Chapter 5: Encounter with a witch 55

Chapter 6: Gifts of the Spirit 78

Chapter 7: Do not marry him! 93

Chapter 8: Followed from Hell (Hades) 106

Chapter 9: Her health for his wealth 115

Chapter 10: Attacks 121

Chapter 11: Cursed Objects and Hosts 144

Chapter 12: The Truth about Spirit Guides 211

Chapter 13: Tattoos and Body Piercing 216

Chapter 14: Cursed Names 232

Chapter 15: Witchcraft 242

Chapter 16: Demonic 272

Chapter 17: Getting back in line with God 293

References 297

Foreword

As a child of 5, I had a vision of me and my mother waiting for my father in a car outside a shop. I saw men coming towards us and they cut my mother with a blade all over her body. They also cut me on my arms and legs.

I did not tell anyone and I did not know what to do at that young age. It all felt very real as I was awake. This was actually one of the very first visions that I can remember. I know now that it was a vision because when I looked at my arms and at my mother we were un-harmed.

From this day it seemed that everything was wrong with us. Everything that was bad was happening to us. I will not discuss this in detail but I can assure you that if you have a calling on you Satan will attack you from very young to make sure you do not walk into that calling. He will do anything to stop you.

Today I teach my grandchildren how to rebuke this type of visions and I ask them what they dreamt about. Why? Because this is the medium Satan use to attack innocent victims.

I got born again at the age of 9 but being in an Orthodox church I did not get the spiritual food that I needed to grow. So in short about twenty years back I was just like every other "Christian" that believed that because I am a child of God and going to church every Sunday nothing bad will happen to me. Satan can do nothing to me and so on.

Surprise! That is exactly what Satan wants you to belief.

There are three categories of people:
- People that are possessed
- People that are oppressed
- People who are ignorant of witchcraft attacks.

God already showed me that this book will cause a big disturbance in the Spiritual World as well as in the physical world. Satan does not want this information to get into the world. So he will use many people to say bad things about this book and even about me. I know I am a sinner and that I made mistakes in the past, but I am no longer that person I am a new person through Jesus Christ. So here is a word to all that want to attack me because of this book that God told me to write to   inform the world.

I was taught by God's Spirit the Holy Spirit in each and every situation, so if you have a problem with the way I dealt with it, take it to God. God told me to write the book to inform the world of what Satan is capable of.

My people are destroyed for lack of knowledge: because thou hast rejected knowledge, I will also reject thee, that thou shalt be no priest to me: seeing thou hast forgotten the law of thy God, I will also forget thy children.

Hosea 4:6

God through His Spirit told me to teach the entire world how to protect them and I will be obedient to my Heavenly Father.

This book is not to judge you on what you are doing or what others are doing. This book has been written as guidelines of what not to do.

God the Father is very clear that we should only serve Him and that we cannot serve Him and hold Satan's hand.

You cannot call yourself a Christian and curse or send witchcraft to another person. You are lying to say that you are a Christian because you are in fact a witch if you do this.

The Bible tells us. If we lie Satan is our father as he is the father of all lies. Yes even a "white lie".

It is your choice what you do with your life. God will never take your freewill away, but just note that you've been informed of the truth.

All scripture are from the New King James Bible unless otherwise stated.

Preface

There is so much in life that we overlook or take for granted simply because of a lack of knowledge and at times through simple ignorance. It is human nature to constantly develop ourselves physically, emotionally and spiritually. And this book comes as a welcomed relief to not only new believers in Christ but also to everyday believers, church leaders, teachers and mentors. It has been put together purely through the calling of our Lord to lead His children down the paths of His righteousness. After all, the Lord is our shepherd (Psalm 23) and He chooses various means and ways to speak to His beloved children.

This book reveals real life situations and experiences of non-believers and believers who have been exposed to attacks and oppression by the enemy by and through so many mediums. Every chapter in this book proves that the bible is the living and breathing work of God. It is a weapon given to us by the Lord to ward off and fight the enemy. And using the blood of Jesus to cover yourself and your loved ones including your home etc. is not something to be taken lightly.

There IS POWER in the BLOOD of Jesus!!! You better believe it!

So the next time you choose to shrug off a weird or bad dream, think again... the first chapter provides insight into visions and dreams to make you aware that the enemy is still at work even when you are asleep. Thereafter you are taken on a journey into the pews of the church. Is a church a holy place where the enemy cannot enter? Do you really know your pastor, what about the people sitting next to you in church...? Everything is not always as it seems and you will see from real life testimony that we have to test everything as believers in Christ.

A real eye opener is the chapter on the majestic eagle and how it relates to our spiritual lives. It truly opens our eyes to the wisdom of God. Amazing how a beautiful piece of scripture can impart so much knowledge...

Surely you have heard of witches right? Ever encountered a real one? You are taken on real life encounters and get to hear of how God protects His children using angels, after all He said He would never leave us... In addition you will learn that a gift may not always just be a gift. You will be shown what the true world of the occult and witchcraft involves, including symbols, signs and more... but most importantly you will learn what you need to do to protect yourself, your loved ones and your home from coming under attack. Also, how simple items in your home can be hosts for the enemy to enter your life and cause upheaval, chaos. Something as simple as a candle can open the door for the enemy to enter your home... don't be fooled dear friends.

What about a name, what is in a name? Well you might be surprised to learn that a name may not just be a name after you have the read the book. The enemy can keep you oppressed because of a name!!! In addition you will read about real life demonic attacks, why deliverance is not something any church or pastor can just perform and why it is important to not open yourself up to further attacks by the enemy.

The purpose of the book is to show you that the world is not all it seems to be, that we need to be extremely vigilant as believers and not expose ourselves or our innocent children to attacks of the enemy. The enemy is the king of deceit and can even attack your household through a fairy tale... he can distort and manipulate your thoughts especially if you are not aware of the truth because of your lack of knowledge. The bible tells us clearly,

"For we wrestle not **against flesh and blood**,
but **against** principalities, **against** powers, **against** the rulers of the darkness of this world, **against** spiritual wickedness in high places."
Ephesians 6:11-13

So empower yourself with the word of God, learn about the fruits of the Spirit and share this book with your friends and family. The only way is Jesus but we are given free will and we have to make the decision to serve Him and only Him and follow the winding road that leads to eternity. Do not let the enemy blind side you, read the chapter on repentance and pray the prayers given to you in this book to release yourself and your family from bondage.

"Trust in the Lord with all thine heart; and **lean not** unto thine **own understanding**. In all thy ways acknowledge him, and he shall direct thy paths."
Proverbs 3:4-7

Leeanne Naicker

Hélèné Fulton

Introduction

What is a Born Again Christian?

The New Birth

3 There was a man of the Pharisees named Nicodemus, a ruler of the Jews. ² This man came to Jesus by night and said to Him, "Rabbi, we know that You are a teacher come from God; for no one can do these signs that You do unless God is with him."
³ Jesus answered and said to him, "Most assuredly, I say to you, unless one is born again, he cannot see the kingdom of God."
⁴ Nicodemus said to Him, "How can a man be born when he is old? Can he enter a second time into his mother's womb and be born?"
⁵ Jesus answered, "Most assuredly, I say to you, unless one is born of water and the Spirit, he cannot enter the kingdom of God. ⁶ That which is born of the flesh is flesh, and that which is born of the Spirit is spirit. ⁷ Do not marvel that I said to you, 'You must be born again.' ⁸ The wind blows where it wishes, and you hear the sound of it, but cannot tell where it comes from and where it goes. So is everyone who is born of the Spirit."
⁹ Nicodemus answered and said to Him, "How can these things be?"
¹⁰ Jesus answered and said to him, "Are you the teacher of Israel, and do not know these things? ¹¹ Most assuredly, I say to you, We speak what We know and testify what We have seen, and you do not receive Our witness. ¹² If I have told you earthly things and you do not believe, how will you believe if I tell you heavenly things? ¹³ No one has ascended to heaven but He who came down from heaven, *that is,* the Son of Man who is in heaven. ¹⁴ And as Moses lifted up the serpent in the wilderness, even so must the Son of Man be lifted up, ¹⁵ that whoever believes in Him should not perish but have eternal life. ¹⁶ For God so loved the world that He gave His only begotten Son, that whoever believes in Him should not perish but have everlasting life. ¹⁷ For God did not send His Son into the world to condemn the world, but that the world through Him might be saved.

Witchcraft in the Church

[18] "He who believes in Him is not condemned; but he who does not believe is condemned already, because he has not believed in the name of the only begotten Son of God. [19] And this is the condemnation, that the light has come into the world, and men loved darkness rather than light, because their deeds were evil. [20] For everyone practicing evil hates the light and does not come to the light, lest his deeds should be exposed. [21] But he who does the truth comes to the light, that his deeds may be clearly seen, that they have been done in God."

John 3:1-21

Nicodemus was a theological professor and a member in parliament, who paid his tithe from all his income, who fasted two days a week, who prayed two hours a day. And Jesus asked him: *"Are you the teacher of Israel, and do not know these things?*

Even today ¾ of the preachers are not born again and does not even know what it means. And they are the ones teaching others the gospel.

It is easy to say that I believe in the Bible. It is easy to say I know the Bible. It is very easy to say I'm a Christian but do you really have it in your heart?

You might be a very good person doing wonderful deeds for your fellow man but have you really been born again!

Are you a new person in Jesus Christ?

Are you willing to let Jesus Christ control your life to totally give yourself over to Him?

Hélèné Fulton

Jesus did not say you ought to be born again He said **you have be** born again if you want to enter the kingdom of God.

You cannot just do the things to show you're a Christian; you need to know the Christ Himself.

Jesus said this because He knows your heart right. He knows you say you love Him but he knows that your heart belongs to business or pleasure or something else.

All the sins you're doing each day comes from within. It starts from the heart and once it reaches the mind you're already making plans to fulfil that desire.

A lot of people supporting the under privilege, but some people are doing it to be seen by others. God looks at what's inside your heart. Don't please people please God.

The phrase "born again" literally means "born from above." Nicodemus had a real need. He needed a change of his heart - a spiritual transformation. New birth, being born again, is an act of God whereby eternal life is imparted to the person who believes indicates that "born again" also carries the idea "to become children of God" through trust in Jesus Christ.

[17] Therefore, if anyone is in Christ, he is a new creation; old things have passed away; behold, all things have become new.

2 Corinthians 5:17

[5] not by works of righteousness which we have done, but according to His mercy He saved us, through the washing of regeneration and renewing of the Holy Spirit,

Titus 3:5

Witchcraft in the Church

³ Blessed be the God and Father of our Lord Jesus Christ, who according to His abundant mercy has begotten us again to a living hope through the resurrection of Jesus Christ from the dead,

1 Peter 1:3

²⁹ If you know that He is righteous, you know that everyone who practices righteousness is born of Him.

1 John 2:29

⁹ Whoever has been born of God does not sin, for His seed remains in him; and he cannot sin, because he has been born of God.

1 John 3:9

⁷ Beloved, let us love one another, for love is of God; and everyone who loves is born of God and knows God.

1 John 4:7

¹ Whoever believes that Jesus is the Christ is born of God, and everyone who loves Him who begot also loves him who is begotten of Him. ² By this we know that we love the children of God, when we love God and keep His commandments. ³ For this is the love of God, that we keep His commandments. And His commandments are not burdensome. ⁴ For whatever is born of God overcomes the world. And this is the victory that has overcome the world—our faith.

1 John 5:1-4

¹⁸ We know that whoever is born of God does not sin; but he who has been born of God keeps himself, and the wicked one does not touch him.

1 John 5:18

Hélèné Fulton

[12] But as many as received Him, to them He gave the right to become children of God, to those who believe in His name: [13] who were born, not of blood, nor of the will of the flesh, nor of the will of man, but of God.

John 1:12-13

[17] Therefore, if anyone is in Christ, he is a new creation; old things have passed away; behold, all things have become new.

2 Corinthians 5:17

If you have never trusted in the Lord Jesus Christ as your Saviour, will you hear the Holy Spirit as He speaks to you? Will you hear the Holy Spirit when He warns you of danger? You need to be born again. Will you pray the prayer of repentance and become a new creation in Jesus Christ today?

[12] But as many as received Him, to them He gave the right to become children of God, to those who believe in His name: [13] who were born, not of blood, nor of the will of the flesh, nor of the will of man, but of God.

John 1:12-13

Remember you do not have to change or wait until you think you are worthy to accept Jesus. God wants you as His own just the way you are. Once you said the prayer God will through His Spirit, the Holy Spirit start His work in you. So many people think that they first needs to change or that they are too big a sinner to be a child of God. Trust me once you say this prayer, God forgives you completely, and He remembers your sin no more.

Yes Satan will try and tell you differently but then tell the devil to get lost because God has never and will never lie to you.

The devil is the father of all lies.

If you are ready then say the prayer below with a sincere heart to accept Jesus Christ as your Lord and Saviour today?

The Prayer that will change Your Eternal Destiny

"Father, I acknowledge that Jesus died for my sins on the cross. Father God please forgive me all of my sins and wash me as white as snow with the Blood of Jesus Christ. Lord Jesus, come into my life. Give me a new heart with new desires. And by Your Spirit, give me the power to live a life that is pleasing to You. Father please fill me with the Holy Spirit. Thank you for forgiving me as You promised. Thank You for the gift of eternal Life."
Amen

Congratulations and welcome to the family of God. No matter what you've done in your life, you've received a full pardon in God's eyes. That's how easy it is for you. But it was not free - it cost God the life of His beloved Son, Jesus Christ in your place. Just thank Him for loving you so much.

You are now a born again believer. Write down this day as you never want to forget this date.

Chapter 1: Visions & Dreams

And it shall come to pass in the last days, says God,
That I will pour out of My Spirit on all flesh;
Your sons and your daughters shall prophesy,
Your young men shall see visions,
Your old men shall dream dreams.

Acts 2:17

Visions:
A vision is simply defined as "being able to see..."
The Bible shows us that God relayed His messages through the power of the Holy Spirit, to His chosen servants by visions and dreams. These messages were also given to the apostles and prophets in various books of the bible.

Dreams:
Defined as a series of thoughts, images, and sensations occurring in a person's mind during sleep.
Dreams usually take place during deep sleep or a REM cycle. REM - Rapid Eye Movement.

Visions are a unique and special way in which God speaks to us. God speaks to His people through different kinds of visions. To receive visions is a gift from the Lord.
I have never had a vision based on something I was thinking about. It was always something totally different.

Very early in my walk with the Lord, He told me to write everything down so I always keep a notebook ready.

Witchcraft in the Church

Visions are sometimes warnings from God and if you are a baby Christian I would suggest that you ask a mature born again Christian to assist you with understanding your visions. At the end of the book are my contact details so you are more than welcome to email me if you need assistance.

About Visions

You can experience different visions at any time

- Visions happen whilst you are awake.
- Some visions looks like photographs. Sometimes you will get more than one photograph that follows each other, one after the other. Sometimes it comes very fast. It stays just long enough for me to notice and then it is gone. This can happen with my eyes open or closed.
- Some photograph looks alive. The photograph is alive. Almost like a movie in a photograph.
- I had visions that looks like a movie are playing right in front of me. Complete with soundtrack.
- Sometimes I could feel all the people's emotions, the good and the bad, emotions and feelings. These are difficult.
- Sometimes I'm at a scene but not part of the scene.
- I had visions where time stood still.
- I had visions were my spiritual eyes were open to see what God wants me to see.
- I had visions where the one will follow on the other to complete the picture that God wants me to see.

Hélèné Fulton
About Dreams

For God may speak in one way, or in another,
Yet man does not perceive it.
In a dream, in a vision of the night,
When deep sleep falls upon men,
While slumbering on their beds,
Then He opens the ears of men,
And seals their instruction.
In order to turn man *from his* deed,
And conceal pride from man,
He keeps back his soul from the Pit,
And his life from perishing by the sword.

Job 33:14-18

If you take dreams away from the Bible it would lose vital components, and yet many do not remember their dreams today. Those people that remember do not take it seriously.

If you cannot remember you cannot make use of it as the Lord intended. Everyone dreams even though some would deny because they cannot remember. Your dream should determine your prayers in the morning.
Dreaming of that sexy hunk or gorgeous girl that you wish you can go out with might not be so innocent.
Sex in the dream (activities of incubus and succubus, spiritual husbands and spiritual wives) food and drinks in the dream, beasts in the dream, particularly serpents are clear indications of what lies ahead in near and far future. Dreams can also reveal what has happened in the past so that you can renounce and break it.

Even a dream that might appear innocent to you might have meaning in the spiritual world.

Witchcraft in the Church

The dreaming realm is a realm of spiritual warfare. God works through dreams, but Satan always counterfeits everything, so you can be sure that he is also working through dreams.
Satan is a liar and a deceiver. One of his ways to carry out his evil plans is to counterfeit the good things of God so that people are fooled into thinking it is God and not Satan.

You are of *your* father the devil, and the desires of your father you want to do. He was a murderer from the beginning, and does not stand in the truth, because there is no truth in him. When he speaks a lie, he speaks from his own *resources,* for he is a liar and the father of it.

John 8:44

Let love be without hypocrisy. Abhor what is evil. Cling to what is good.

Romans 12:9

Now when the thousand years have expired, Satan will be released from his prison [8] and will go out to deceive the nations which are in the four corners of the earth, Gog and Magog, to gather them together to battle, whose number *is* as the sand of the sea.

Revelation 20:7-8

The devil, who deceived them, was cast into the lake of fire and brimstone where the beast and the false prophet *are.* And they will be tormented day and night forever and ever.

Revelation 20:10

Satan will counterfeit almost anything. Let's look at some of the things Satan counterfeits.

Hélèné Fulton

God send prophets to proclaim His word. Satan sends false prophets.

Beloved, do not believe every spirit, but test the spirits, whether they are of God; because many false prophets have gone out into the world.
1 John 4:1

Then many false prophets will rise up and deceive many.
Matthew 24:11

For false christs and false prophets will rise and show great signs and wonders to deceive, if possible, even the elect.
Matthew 24:24

"Beware of false prophets, who come to you in sheep's clothing, but inwardly they are ravenous wolves.[16] You will know them by their fruits. Do men gather grapes from thornbushes or figs from thistles?
Matthew 7:15-16

When God gives us teachers to teach His word Satan sends false teachers.

But there were also false prophets among the people, even as there will be false teachers among you, who will secretly bring in destructive heresies, even denying the Lord who bought them, *and* bring on themselves swift destruction. [2] And many will follow their destructive ways, because of whom the way of truth will be blasphemed. [3] By covetousness they will exploit you with deceptive words; for a long time their judgment has not been idle, and their destruction does not slumber.
2 Peter 2:1-3

Witchcraft in the Church

Now the Spirit expressly says that in latter times some will depart from the faith, giving heed to deceiving spirits and doctrines of demons, ² speaking lies in hypocrisy, having their own conscience seared with a hot iron, ³ forbidding to marry, *and commanding* to abstain from foods which God created to be received with thanksgiving by those who believe and know the truth.

1 Timothy 4:1-3

Whoever transgresses and does not abide in the doctrine of Christ does not have God. He who abides in the doctrine of Christ has both the Father and the Son. ¹⁰ If anyone comes to you and does not bring this doctrine, do not receive him into your house nor greet him; ¹¹ for he who greets him shares in his evil deeds.

2 John 1:9-11

But you have departed from the way;
You have caused many to stumble at the law.
You have corrupted the covenant of Levi,"
Says the LORD of hosts.
⁹ "Therefore I also have made you contemptible and base
Before all the people,
Because you have not kept My ways
But have shown partiality in the law."

Malachi 2:8-9

I marvel that you are turning away so soon from Him who called you in the grace of Christ, to a different gospel, ⁷ which is not another; but there are some who trouble you and want to pervert the gospel of Christ. ⁸ But even if we, or an angel from heaven, preach any other gospel to you than what we have preached to you, let him be accursed. ⁹ As we have said before, so now I say again, if anyone preaches any other gospel to you than what you have received, let him be accursed.

Galatians 1:6-9

Hélèné Fulton

The Bible tells us that Jesus Christ is the Light of the world.

This man came for a witness, to bear witness of the Light, that all through him might believe. ⁸ He was not that Light, but *was sent* to bear witness of that Light. ⁹ That was the true Light which gives light to every man coming into the world.

John 1:7-9

Then Jesus spoke to them again, saying, "I am the light of the world. He who follows Me shall not walk in darkness, but have the light of life."

John 8:12

A light to *bring* revelation to the Gentiles,
And the glory of Your people Israel."

Luke 2:32

Then Jesus said to them, "A little while longer the light is with you. Walk while you have the light, lest darkness overtake you; he who walks in darkness does not know where he is going.³⁶ While you have the light, believe in the light, that you may become sons of light." These things Jesus spoke, and departed, and was hidden from them.

John 12:35-36

Satan appears as an "angel of light".

And no wonder! For Satan himself transforms himself into an **angel of light**.

2 Corinthians 11:14

God is a triune being (the trinity). The Bible from Genesis to Revelation depicts God as being triune in nature, that He has three forms or three ways of revealing Himself in the deepest and most intimate way and means!

The Bible, God's Word, proclaims that there is ONE God, Who has revealed Himself to mankind in three distinct

Persons; namely, God the Father, God the Son and God the Holy Spirit. Although the term "Trinity" is not found in the Scriptures, the word "Godhead" most certainly is — in 3 places!

⁴ "Hear, O Israel: The LORD our God, the LORD *is* one!
Deuteronomy 6:4

¹⁹ because what may be known of God is manifest in them, for God has shown *it* to them. ²⁰ For since the creation of the world His invisible *attributes* are clearly seen, being understood by the things that are made, *even* His eternal power and Godhead, so that they are without excuse
Romans 1:19-20

Some people, such as Muslims foolishly claim that they belief in the Godhead aka, Trinity, means worship of three gods (polytheism). This simply reflects their woeful ignorance of the Word of God. The LORD our God is ONE Lord (Deuteronomy 6:4); but He does exist in three Persons, i.e., a Trinity.

²⁹ Forasmuch then as we are the offspring of God, we ought not to think that the Godhead is like unto gold, or silver, or stone, graven by art and man's device.
Acts 17:29 (KJ)

⁹ For in him dwelleth all the fulness of the Godhead bodily.
Colossians 2:9 (KJ)

God the Father

God the Father is the "Big Boss". It was God's idea to create man. God is the Thinker. God is the Operator.

God the Son (Jesus Christ)

Jesus Christ is the administrator, the doer.

Beware lest anyone cheat you through philosophy and empty deceit, according to the tradition of men, according to the basic principles of the world, and not according to Christ. [9] For in Him dwells all the fullness of the Godhead bodily; [10] and you are complete in Him, who is the head of all principality and power.

Colossians 2:8-10

God the Holy Spirit

Holy Spirit is the Power. It is His power that brings the ministering manifestations.

Holy Spirit is the third person of the Godhead and is as much God as the Father and Jesus Christ the Son are.
The Holy Spirit is not just a mere influence or attitude – He is truly God, a divine personality.

Jesus Promises Another Helper
[15] "If you love Me, keep My commandments. [16] And I will pray the Father, and He will give you another Helper, that He may abide with you forever—[17] the Spirit of truth, whom the world cannot receive, because it neither sees Him nor knows Him; but you know Him, for He dwells with you and will be in you. [18] I will not leave you orphans; I will come to you.

Indwelling of the Father and the Son
[19] "A little while longer and the world will see Me no more, but you will see Me. Because I live, you will live also. [20] At that day you will know that I *am* in My Father, and you in Me, and I in you. [21] He who has My commandments and keeps them, it is he who loves Me. And he who

Witchcraft in the Church

loves Me will be loved by My Father, and I will love him and manifest Myself to him."

²² Judas (not Iscariot) said to Him, "Lord, how is it that You will manifest Yourself to us, and not to the world?"

²³ Jesus answered and said to him, "If anyone loves Me, he will keep My word; and My Father will love him, and We will come to him and make Our home with him. ²⁴ He who does not love Me does not keep My words; and the word which you hear is not Mine but the Father's who sent Me.

The Gift of His Peace

²⁵ "These things I have spoken to you while being present with you. ²⁶ But the Helper, the Holy Spirit, whom the Father will send in My name, He will teach you all things, and bring to your remembrance all things that I said to you. ²⁷ Peace I leave with you, My peace I give to you; not as the world gives do I give to you. Let not your heart be troubled, neither let it be afraid. ²⁸ You have heard Me say to you, 'I am going away and coming *back* to you.' If you loved Me, you would rejoice because I said,[b] 'I am going to the Father,' for My Father is greater than I.

²⁹ "And now I have told you before it comes, that when it does come to pass, you may believe. ³⁰ I will no longer talk much with you, for the ruler of this world is coming, and he has nothing in Me. ³¹ But that the world may know that I love the Father, and as the Father gave Me commandment, so I do. Arise, let us go from here.

John 14:15-31

You feel the Power (Holy Spirit) not the presence.
Salvation is the presence of the Lord, the Glory of God.

Jesus Christ is the Glory of God in the flesh.

But you shall receive power when the Holy Spirit has come upon you; and you shall be witnesses to Me in Jerusalem, and in all Judea and Samaria, and to the end of the earth.

Acts 1:8

The "unholy trinity" form at Armageddon by Satan

And I saw three unclean spirits like frogs *coming* out of the mouth of the dragon, out of the mouth of the beast, and out of the mouth of the false prophet.

Revelation 16:13

Satan always takes God's word and twists it to serve his purpose.

Then Jesus was led up by the Spirit into the wilderness to be tempted by the devil. ² And when He had fasted forty days and forty nights, afterward He was hungry. ³ Now when the tempter came to Him, he said, "If You are the Son of God, command that these stones become bread."
⁴ But He answered and said, "It is written, 'Man shall not live by bread alone, but by every word that proceeds from the mouth of God.'"
⁵ Then the devil took Him up into the holy city, set Him on the pinnacle of the temple, ⁶ and said to Him, "If You are the Son of God, throw Yourself down. For it is written:
'He shall give His angels charge over you,'
and,
'In *their* hands they shall bear you up,
Lest you dash your foot against a stone.'"
⁷ Jesus said to him, "It is written again, 'You shall not tempt the LORD your God.'"
⁸ Again, the devil took Him up on an exceedingly high mountain, and showed Him all the kingdoms of the world and their glory.
⁹ And he said to Him, "All these things I will give You if You will fall down and worship me."
¹⁰ Then Jesus said to him, "Away with you, Satan! For it is written, 'You shall worship the LORD your God, and Him only you shall serve.'"

Witchcraft in the Church

> [11] Then the devil left Him, and behold, angels came and ministered to Him.
>
> **Matthew 4:1-11**

Satan also took God's spiritual gifts and causes them to be misused to create confusion.

Jesus is called the Lion of Judah.

> But one of the elders said to me, "Do not weep. Behold, the Lion of the tribe of Judah, the Root of David, has prevailed to open the scroll and to loose its seven seals."
>
> **Revelation 5:5**

Satan is compared to a "roaring lion" (1 Pet 5:8).

> Be sober, be vigilant; because your adversary the devil walks about like a roaring lion, seeking whom he may devour.
>
> **1 Peter 5:8**

I had a vision from God about 3 years back to help me understand this better.

In the vision I saw the Lion and under His feet I saw a white mouse. The mouse could not move but was alive.

Jesus Christ has defeated Satan 2000 years ago on the cross. Satan however still tries to attack and he succeed if we are not born again and if we do not protect ourselves with the Blood of Jesus and the full Armour of God.

When we are protected and are born again Satan is like a little white mouse.

¹³ Therefore take up the whole armor of God, that you may be able to withstand in the evil day, and having done all, to stand.
¹⁴ Stand therefore, having girded your waist with truth, having put on the breastplate of righteousness, ¹⁵ and having shod your feet with the preparation of the gospel of peace; ¹⁶ above all, taking the shield of faith with which you will be able to quench all the fiery darts of the wicked one. ¹⁷ And take the helmet of salvation, and the sword of the Spirit, which is the word of God; ¹⁸ praying always with all prayer and supplication in the Spirit, being watchful to this end with all perseverance and supplication for all the saints— ¹⁹ and for me, that utterance may be given to me, that I may open my mouth boldly to make known the mystery of the gospel, ²⁰ for which I am an ambassador in chains; that in it I may speak boldly, as I ought to speak.

Ephesians 6:13-20

Jesus instituted "communion," and Satan falsifies it.

The cup of blessing which we bless, is it not the communion of the blood of Christ? The bread which we break, is it not the communion of the body of Christ? ¹⁷ For we, *though* many, are one bread *and* one body; for we all partake of that one bread.
¹⁸ Observe Israel after the flesh: Are not those who eat of the sacrifices partakers of the altar? ¹⁹ What am I saying then? That an idol is anything, or what is offered to idols is anything? ²⁰ Rather, that the things which the Gentiles sacrifice they sacrifice to demons and not to God, and I do not want you to have fellowship with demons. ²¹ You cannot drink the cup of the Lord and the cup of demons; you cannot partake of the Lord's table and of the table of demons. ²² Or do we provoke the Lord to jealousy? Are we stronger than He?

1 Corinthians 10:16-22

So how do we know what is of God and what is counterfeit? We must diligently read and study God's word, and know it so well, that when we hear or see something that doesn't line up with the Bible, we will know it instantly. If we don't spend time becoming familiar with God's word, as well as spending time with God in prayer, we are likely to fall prey to Satan's deceptions.

Protect your dream life before you sleep using the blood of Jesus Christ, the full armour of God and the fire of the Holy Spirit.

To the Holy Spirit belongs the interpretation of dreams. He reveals the deep and secret things.

Please get in touch with us by email to know more about your dreams.

If you cannot remember your dreams say this prayer every night before you go to bed.

Father God I know that I am dreaming but I cannot remember any of my dreams. Father I pray that You will let me dream the dreams that I have forgotten and that is very important again. Father I also pray that from this day forth that You will let me remember all my dreams the morning after I have dream them. I pray this in the name of Jesus Christ. Amen

Chapter 2: Who is the Church?

When answering this Question I think we need to look at the widely accepted opinion;

"**God, who made the world and everything in it, since He is Lord of heaven and earth, does not dwell in temples made with hands.** [25] Nor is He worshiped with men's hands, as though He needed anything, since He gives to all life, breath, and all things.

Acts 17:24-25

We also read in the Bible

Then news of these things came to the **ears of the church** in Jerusalem, and they sent out Barnabas to go as far as Antioch.

Acts 11:22

Saul was making havoc of the church by persecuting God's people. It is clear from the scriptural verse below that Saul did not drag a building like a Temple to prison.

Now Saul was consenting to his death.
At that time a great persecution arose against the church which was at Jerusalem; and they were all scattered throughout the regions of Judea and Samaria, except the apostles. [2] And devout men carried Stephen *to his burial,* and made great lamentation over him.
[3] **As for Saul, he made havoc of the church, entering every house**, and dragging off men and women, committing *them* to prison.
[4] Therefore those who were scattered went everywhere preaching the word.

Acts 8:1-4

Witchcraft in the Church

We read of the church in the house of Priscilla and Aquilla

Greet **Priscilla and Aquila**, my **fellow workers in Christ Jesus**, [4] who risked their own necks for my life, to whom not only I give thanks, but also all the churches of the Gentiles. [5] Likewise *greet* **the church that is in their house**.
Greet my beloved Epaenetus, who is the firstfruits of Achaia to Christ.

Romans 16:3-5

Paul gathering the church together at Antioch.

Now when they had come and **gathered the church together**, they reported all that God had done with them, and that He had opened the door of faith to the Gentiles.

Acts 14:27

Clearly from the verse above we can see that the church is not a building. Is it possible to gather buildings together?

Membership in the church is determined by neither people, preacher nor priest or any other 5 fold ministry but by the Lord.

And He Himself gave some *to be* apostles, some prophets, some evangelists, and some pastors and teachers, [12] for the equipping of the saints for the work of ministry, for the edifying of the body of Christ,

Ephesians 4:11-12

Hélèné Fulton

...praising God and having favor with all the people. And **the Lord added to the church daily those who were being saved.**
Acts 2:47

So clearly from the verse above you cannot join.

For I am not ashamed of the gospel of Christ, for it is the **power of God to salvation for everyone who believes**, for the Jew first and also for the Greek.
Romans 1:16

Moreover, brethren, I declare to you the gospel which I preached to you, which also you received and in which you stand, ² by which also you are saved, if you hold fast that word which I preached to you—unless you believed in vain.
³ For I delivered to you first of all that which I also received: that Christ died for our sins according to the Scriptures, ⁴ and that He was buried, and that He rose again the third day according to the Scriptures,
1 Corinthians 15:1-4

Those who are "the church" are perfectly organized, having Christ as their "head" and a position that is God-ordained.

And He put all *things* under His feet, and gave Him *to be* head over all *things* to the church, ²³ which is His body, the fullness of Him who fills all in all.
Ephesians 1:22-23

But now **God has set the members, each one of them, in the body just as He pleased.**
1 Corinthians 12:18

What spiritual ignorance is shown by any of these who believe they need a human "organizer" or that they can improve upon the work of the infinitely wise and powerful God.

Witchcraft in the Church

> And He Himself gave some *to be* apostles, some prophets, some evangelists, and some pastors and teachers,
>
> **Ephesians 4:11**

They limit and frustrate the work of these men and women when they "call" or "appoint" pastors or teachers of their choice or when a pastor suddenly decide he is now a prophet or an apostle or a bishop.

Recently, there has been a lot of conflict concerning this matter. As a messenger of the Most High God, I have been instructed to sound the trumpet, and engage the enemy whose goal is to destroy and erase this from the plan of God in the body of Christ! I am not here to entice you with man's wisdom, but rather to call this nation and the church to repentance!

Organizations have tried to silence the ordinances of God, to pursue their own agendas, and for that, they will face Godly judgement just as I will be judged for my mistakes.

I pray that all will come in humbleness before God, ask God to forgive them and guide them into the truth, His truth.

The fivefold ministry is one of the greatest keys to any successful ministry. The ministries, who do not operate in all five, are damaging the growth of the body of Christ!

A ministry who does not acknowledge the entire Fivefold ministry and who does not want Teachers, Evangelists,

Hélèné Fulton

Prophets and Apostles in their ministry have one or more of the following hidden agendas:

- They don't have an understanding of each one of these offices.
- Control issues within the ministry. The pastor might even have the spirit of Diotrephes.
  When a ministry has the fivefold ministry in operation, that organizations are no longer are in control. The Pastors are no longer in control. God is in control!

I am briefly going to explain each office.

In Ephesians 4:11, each one of these offices is separated by semi-colons. Because each office separated means that it is exclusive from the others. Notice that Pastors and Teachers are together? Why? Pastors and Teachers belong together. No man is fit to be a Pastor who cannot also teach, and the Teacher needs the knowledge which Pastoral experience gives.

Ephesians 4:12 says "For the perfecting of the saints..." This does not mean that the saints *cannot* reach perfection *unless* there is a fivefold ministry in the church? "For the work of the ministry..." This is to perfect *the saints* so that they can work in the ministry that they've been called in! "For the **edifying** (building) of the body of Christ;"

Apostles pioneer churches (remember who is the church). They build them from the ground up. They establish and restore them. They have special inspiration from God, and are given supreme authority over the churches (this is why denominations have ruled them out). True Apostles are accredited by signs and miracles following their ministry (self-proclaimed "Apostles" do not), Apostles have an unlimited commission to preach the Gospel. Apostles oversee and are responsible for every church that they have pioneered. Now bear in mind that you are the church and not the building you worship in. God will take an Apostle through all the other offices because they must know and understand what these offices are about in order to teach the body of Christ. To life a holy life is very important to the Apostle appointed by God, as they never want to disappoint God.

God will use Apostles (male and female) and Prophets to reveal or confirm a person's calling.

To the churches that claim that there cannot be any apostles today. Think again. The Apostle Paul was an Apostle almost 20 years after Jesus Christ ascended to Heaven.

11 to which I was appointed a preacher, an apostle, and a teacher of the Gentiles.

2 Timothy 1:11

Prophets (male and female) are called by God alone. Prophets work with the guidance of the Holy Spirit.

Prophets are somewhat on a planet of their own. They are eccentric, somewhat weird to church and society, and are oftentimes abandoned by man because of their being misunderstood by mainstream religious groups.

True Prophets of God are dealt with by God and God alone. They are oftentimes trained in ministry alone, with some guidance by other true Prophets or Apostles appointed by God over them.

False "Prophets" are mainly 'soothsayers", often known as a 'slithering tongued serpent', tickling the ears to gain your trust. This world is full of them!

True Prophets of God can operate as an Evangelist, Pastor or Teacher. Prophets are also followed by signs and miracles when directed by God to do so. They only speak the Word of God, and are assisted by God to carry out the Prophet's assignment.

A true Prophet of God lives a very holy life.

Apostles and Prophets oftentimes walk together. They are both over the Evangelist, Pastor and Teacher.

The **Evangelist** draws the crowds and all that matters to them is to save the lost souls. Evangelists travel, and are constantly on the road, except for the time of 'refreshing' or encouragement from other ministries within the body of Christ. The Evangelist works hand-in-hand with the Pastor and Teacher.

A **Pastors** main job is to "shepherd" the flock. A true pastor will visit his congregation, do hospital visits. His "sheep" is very important to him. If you have ever watched the series 7TH Heaven. Eric Camden, the pastor in this series shows all the qualities of a true pastor. A pastor will also do a lot of Bible study in order to teach his congregation.
PS: Your pastors title might be reverend, minister, priest etc.

Witchcraft in the Church

Teachers teach foundational truths of the Word of God, building the foundation of our faith. Joyce Meyer is an excellent example of a true teacher.

Once again, this is the order of God:
1) Apostles
2) Prophets
3) Evangelists
4) Pastors
5) Teachers

Organizations are formed by man, and not God! Organizations have become man-made empires that have been designed to suppress (control) people

As long as Apostles and Prophets are silenced, then this puts the Pastor the head of the church and not Christ.

This is not about the "power" or position of the calling itself, because the 'higher' the calling, the higher the price, the heavier the burden, and the more the sacrifice. That's just the way it is, trust me! It's about a *true* ministry. A ministry without spot or blemish. A ministry that doesn't experience defeat. A ministry with supernatural POWER! A ministry that is truly called by God Almighty.

Sometimes God takes you through the different callings to teach you. This happens with prophets and apostles. God has taken me through all the callings, some longer than others to teach me so that I will be able to teach others.

Hélèné Fulton

Just in case you've wondered. A Bishop is just an elder over elders.

This is the only church with divine origin and blessing. It alone can fulfil this prayer of the Lord Jesus Christ for all who believe on Him:

that they all may be one, as You, Father, *are* in Me, and I in You; that they also may be one in Us, that the world may believe that You sent Me.

John 17:21

All divisions (denominations and sects) show sinful disregard for the will of God and of the "unity of the Spirit" See scripture below.

Now I plead with you, brethren, by the name of our Lord Jesus Christ, that you all speak the same thing, and *that* there be no divisions among you, but *that* you be perfectly joined together in the same mind and in the same judgment.

1 Corinthians 1:10

And I, brethren, could not speak to you as to spiritual *people* but as to carnal, as to babes in Christ. ² I fed you with milk and not with solid food; for until now you were not able *to receive it,* and even now you are still not able; ³ for you are still carnal. For where *there are* envy, strife, and divisions among you, are you not carnal and behaving like *mere* men? ⁴ For when one says, "I am of Paul," and another, "I *am* of Apollos," are you not carnal?

1 Corinthians 3:1-4

Do you not know that you are the temple of God and *that* the Spirit of God dwells in you? ¹⁷ If anyone defiles the temple of God, God will destroy him. For the temple of God is holy, which *temple* you are.

1 Corinthians 3:16-17

Witchcraft in the Church

> I, therefore, the prisoner of the Lord, beseech you to walk worthy of the calling with which you were called, ² with all lowliness and gentleness, with longsuffering, bearing with one another in love, ³ endeavoring to keep the unity of the Spirit in the bond of peace. ⁴ *There is* one body and one Spirit, just as you were called in one hope of your calling; ⁵ one Lord, one faith, one baptism; ⁶ one God and Father of all, who *is* above all, and through all, and in you all.
>
> **Ephesians 4:1-6**

I think that you will now agree with me that we are the church not the building that we worship in. The church is also called the body of Christ. Unfortunately the body of Christ is very sick as Christians are working against each other and not together as one body. The reason for this is pride. The pastor became too proud and greedy and because of this, souls are being lost.

The church is made of people all over the world who have discovered the love of God as demonstrated by Jesus Christ.

Chapter 3: Hurt by the Church

I was fellowshipping in a church in Durban and I remember the pastor and his wife continuously saying that they are so busy and that they cannot get to all the things they need to do on a daily basis.

On several occasions I have offered my services and help but was always turned down.

During the second month with this church, at one of the Wednesday night services, I was prompted by the Holy Spirit to bless a young mother and her children. Things were really going bad for this mother. Her baby girl was attacked by rats in her apartment and the baby nearly died in hospital. People open your eyes – there is a real need in the world for help. Christians should rather only employ Christians and not become unequally yoked by employing non-believers.

14 Do not be unequally yoked together with unbelievers. For what fellowship has righteousness with lawlessness? And what communion has light with darkness?

2 Corinthians 6:14

Privately I asked the mother to meet me the next day at one of the groceries stores. I did not even tell [1]Jacob, with whom I was married at the time as blessing someone is a private thing between you and that person and God.

Do Good to Please God

---

[1] the name "Jacob" meaning, "trickster, supplanter, heel grabber.
Please note even though the real name was changed for various reasons. The meaning of my ex-husband's name and Jacob remains the same.

Witchcraft in the Church

"Take heed that you do not do your charitable deeds before men, to be seen by them. Otherwise you have no reward from your Father in heaven. 2 Therefore, when you do a charitable deed, do not sound a trumpet before you as the hypocrites do in the synagogues and in the streets, that they may have glory from men. Assuredly, I say to you, they have their reward. 3 But when you do a charitable deed, do not let your left hand know what your right hand is doing, 4 that your charitable deed may be in secret; and your Father who sees in secret will Himself reward you openly.
Matthew 6:1-4

After we left the premises, the lady that I was told to bless by God was so excited that she told the pastors wife about it.

At about 11pm I receive a call from the pastor's wife telling me that I am no longer welcome at their church because if I want to bless someone I need to give them the money and they will bless who they think needs it. This was a shock to me as this is not what the Holy Spirit told me.

My answer to her was that I am sure God will use me at another church where He will place me.

I was very calm saying this to the pastor's wife but after I ended the call I was devastated. I could not believe that I was kicked out of a church because I chose to obey the Holy Spirit.

I was crying for more than a week as I was deeply hurt by the words of this pastor's wife.

Hélèné Fulton

If it was not for God and my love for Him I would have probably never put my foot in another church let alone have my own ministry.

It was around this time that God led me to the following letter that I found on the internet while searching for something completely un-related to pastors or churches.

Forgive Your Pastor

Dear former church member,

"I'm sorry... I was wrong... Please forgive me, if you and I were close enough for me to hold your hand, I would be holding it now. If I could look you in the eyes, that's where I'd be staring. On behalf of every pastor who has ever hurt you, I want to repent.

When it comes to convincing you of just how bad I feel for what I've done, I don't know where to start. I feel like a blind man searching for a starting block.

So much needs to be said. So much needs to be forgiven. I was your pastor, and I hurt you. You trusted me, and I injured you. You saw me as a hero, and I disappointed you.

You thought I should be like Paul and Peter, and you were right. I should have been - but I wasn't. Forgive me for trying to somehow win the lost while I was whipping the saved.

God has been talking with me about my lack of a shepherd's heart and the absence of concern on my behalf. For the first time, I'm feeling grief over the loss of you from the church.

If this is you, by God's amazing grace, allow me to stand as a

Witchcraft in the Church

pastor in the place of the pastor who hurt you and say these words to you; forgive me, I was wrong."

Now let me help you understand where I went wrong. Leading a church is filled with tremendous pressures. When God called me into the ministry I saw only the souls that I would one day preach to.

I never saw in any vision the stacks of phone messages that seem to scream for my return call each day. I never saw the building-committee hassles. I never saw the mortgage-debt headaches. And I certainly never saw the staff disloyalties I would have to face. If I had, I probably would have rejected God's call.

I feel at times so much like Moses. God revealed to him His wondrous plan on a mountain. But while "on the way" to Egypt to deliver Israel, God told him that He would harden Pharaoh's heart. You see, like you, my life and ministry have been tougher than I planned.

And for that reason, I falsely began to feel I had a license to behave selfishly toward you. Forgive me. There were many days I let the fatigue of ministry rule my life as I placed servanthood at the bottom of my priorities. It seemed to be always on those days that we found ourselves interacting. Forgive me.

The power of pride, not the power of the Holy Spirit, has ruled many of my relationships. I was insecure and frustrated so I carried an air of superiority toward you. I can even remember trying to manipulate you from the pulpit with a power glare. How utterly wrong for a shepherd to have behaved that way.

As preachers, we are good with our words - it's our life. I learned early on that I could control people with my words. I now realize this created a wall between us. On several occasions you tried to call me, and I avoided you because I was too prideful to hear what you had to say. You wrote me a letter, but I didn't give it the time of day.

You would see me with my golf clubs and wonder how I had the time to play but not the time to respond to you. I knew exactly what you were thinking, but regretfully, I arrogantly chose to ignore it. Forgive me.

I also feel sorrow because I've created a new dilemma for you. The ball is now in your court. I've asked you for forgiveness, and you must decide if God is big enough to span years of hurt. A wound is actually a temptation - a painful apple offered by Satan to further appease his destructive intent for your life. Don't give him a chance!

Yours pastor.

I later discover that several people including Pastor Koos are very good friends with this pastor and his wife. I then understood that they are serving the same god and not the true God Almighty. Because if you are truly born again, God directs your every footstep and your everyday manner in which you handle things. I do not even get dressed without asking God what He wants me to wear. It is that important to me to always be in line with my Father God and His will for me.

I forgave this pastor and his wife. The minute I have forgiven them God spoke to me through His Spirit telling me that now

Witchcraft in the Church

I am ready to start the ministry that I am called for. God told me to start an online ministry to reach the people that are not helped by their church and those people that do not belong to a church and also the people that have never put a foot inside a church. God said to me that this ministry will reach millions of people.

God showed me in a vision, that many lost souls will be saved from hell and that one day I will see just how many people have been helped through this ministry. This vision looked like a scene from the train stations in a big city like New York. Millions of smiling faces where flashing before my eyes.

I had this vision in August 2010. Immediately after this God said to me that the ministry's name will be Light the World Ministries.

I asked God why Light the World Ministries and not Light of the World Ministries. God answered me and said the Light of the World will shine through Light the World Ministries.

God also showed me the template for the website. On the top right I wanted to add Jesus loves you and God said NO. It should read **God loves you**. I asked why? God said that many people do not know Jesus yet but reading the teachings on the website will lead them to love Jesus and then they will come to the Father through Jesus Christ.

Hélèné Fulton

Then God said that Light the World Ministries will teach the people just how much God loves them. God gave me the following scripture for Light the World Ministries.

For God so loved the world that He gave His only begotten Son, that whoever believes in Him should not perish but have everlasting life.

John 3:16

Then God started to give me the teachings He wanted on the website for the online ministry.

A week later God said to me that you will also help people to be set free from bondage through deliverance. I was shocked as I was afraid of the smallest spider and now God wants me to take on demons. I had no deliverance training and did not even know where to start. God said to me that He will be my teacher through His Spirit. It was at this time that God said I should also start the online Deliverance Ministry.

I entered into a covenant with God that I will always tell the people the truth whether they like it or not.

God gave me the following scripture for the Deliverance Ministry

My people are destroyed for lack of knowledge: because thou hast rejected knowledge, I will also reject thee, that thou shalt be no priest to me: seeing thou hast forgotten the law of thy God, I will also forget thy children.

Hosea 4:6

God said to me I want you to teach my people so that they will be able to resist the devil.

Witchcraft in the Church

God gave me the Template for the deliverance ministry. It was scary. I asked God why this template and He answered: "This is where the people will go if they do not repent." Then God started to give me the teachings that He wanted on the deliverance website.

During the next two months I learned more than I've ever learnt my entire life.

I have included most of what I have been taught by God into my books so that you can learn from it.

Chapter 4: The Fish Eagle

In the beginning of October 2010 I asked God to give me a sign that I am on the right path and that I have heard Him correctly when He told me to start an online ministry, that the articles I am publishing on the website for the ministry are the correct teachings from Him and that I am not being misled by something else like so many other religions out there.

Two weeks later I was driving on the N7 highway between Durban and Pinetown. This is a 3 lane cement highway.

A fish eagle came from the right side and was flying to the front of my vehicle. It was just soaring in front of my car. I could see into its eyes and I remember that this was a huge bird.

Time stood still. I was on a highway and the speed limit was 80km per hour. Cars were passing by but I stood still. I cannot explain it. I was driving but the car was not moving forward, I was captured by this amazing bird. For about 10 minutes I just stared at the bird and the bird looked right into my eyes.

I had my sister's daughter who was 14 at the time with me in the car and we both agreed that the eyes of this bird were the size of a saucer. I remember looking in a bird book later and the fish eagles in the book are not that big.

I knew that it was supernatural. That night I received the following scripture from God.

> "But those who wait on the Lord shall renew their strength; they shall mount up with wings like eagles, they shall run and not be weary, they shall walk and not faint."
>
> **Isaiah 40:31**

I knew that this was God appearing to me through the eagle and whenever God gives me a specific analogy in the Bible, what He wants me to do is to examine what the analogy is all about so that I can fully understand what He is trying to teach me.

The two key words in this verse are that we will mount up with wings **"like eagles."**

> But they that wait upon the LORD shall renew their strength; they shall mount up with wings as eagles; they shall run, and not be weary; and they shall walk, and not faint.
>
> **Isaiah 40:31 (KJV)**

The Original King James Version uses the words **"as eagles."**

I believe God is trying to tell us something when He compares us to eagles in this scriptural verse. I remember when I saw this verse; it really stood out from the page. I then did a study on eagles and their personality traits just to see if there were any personality traits that were inherent in the eagle that God wanted me to have with Him.

After finding out exactly what personality traits eagles do have, I came to the conclusion that God was definitely trying to give me some additional knowledge regarding the qualities He would like me to have in my personality and in my walk and ministry with Him.

The first thing I learned about the eagle is all about how they are able to fly, but mostly on how they are able to **soar** without actually flapping their wings.

Their wings are spread straight out and they are literally soaring with perfect ease on the wind currents.

Eagles are born with big and heavy wings, and part of their survival mechanism they are born with is that they have to learn how to fly without actually flapping their wings. They have to learn how to do this in order to save energy. Eagles can die if they use too much energy flapping their wings during flight as to soaring without flapping their wings.

As a result, what eagles have to learn to do very early on in order to be able to soar without flapping their wings, is to wait for what are called wind thermals to come up on them. A wind thermal is a big gust of wind that will rise up from the atmosphere. Sometimes eagles will remain perched for days before they can catch a good, strong, wind thermal, where they can then launch onto it and combine a mixture of flying and soaring on that strong wind thermal to get them to where they want to go.

God is giving us a very powerful revelation here on how eagles basically fly and soar on these wind thermals.

God is saying we are the eagle and the wings of the eagles represent our faith and belief in God and the wind thermals the eagles fly on represent the Holy Spirit.

God gave me another scripture two days later.

Witchcraft in the Church

Not by might nor by power, but by My Spirit,'
Says the LORD of hosts.

Zechariah 4:6

What God was telling me is that all things will get fully accomplished for Him by the power of the Holy Spirit operating through me, not by my own power or by my own flesh.

Just like the eagle has to learn how to fly all born again, Spirit-filled Christians, have to learn how to fly on the power of the Holy Spirit working in our lives. We have to learn how to walk and fly with the anointing of God.

The anointing of God is the power of the Holy Spirit flowing and operating through us to accomplish what God wants us to do for Him. It is God's power flowing and operating through us. God's power is pure and absolute.

I had to learn 4 very important things in my walk and ministry with God.

1. How to be led by the Holy Spirit
2. How to fully trust Him
3. And how to walk with His anointing operating through me so that I can fully accomplish everything that the Lord is planning for me.
4. How to always obey the Holy Spirit in everything I do.

If you do not learn how to be **led** by the Holy Spirit in your daily life, then you will never find out exactly what

Hélèné Fulton

God is going to call you to do for Him in this life. You will never find out who your true soul mate is going to be, and you will never fulfil the divine destiny to which God has called you.

Just like an eagle has to learn how to **catch the wind thermal** in order to survive, we have to learn how to be **led by the Holy Spirit** on a daily basis so we can fully accomplish everything God will want us to accomplish for Him in our walk with Him.

If God calls someone to be a great evangelist and then leads him to the exact spots where He will want him to work, but that person does not learn how to flow and walk with God's anointing on him, then he will have minimal success in that specific calling. Again, not by our flesh (might) or by our power, but by the power of the Holy Spirit operating through us, is how we will produce good fruits for the Lord.

If we do not have enough faith and belief in God to take flight on the Holy Spirit in order to be led and empowered by Him for service to the Lord, then nothing will ever happen. We will stay in one place, and we will never fulfil the divine destiny that God has already planned out for our lives before we were even born into our mother's womb.

The eagle has to take that big leap off the edge of the cliff in order to be able to fly and soar on those wind thermals. If the eagle does not take flight on those wind thermals when they do come up on him, he will forever stay on the cliff and he will starve to death on the cliff.

In the same way, if we do not take flight on the Holy Spirit and the divine call that God has placed on our lives, our lives will perish right before our very own eyes, as the Bible tells us that God's people will perish without having His specific vision for their lives.

Sooner or later, every single Christian will have to make that big choice for their lives. Who will they decide to serve and follow in this life? Do they follow and serve their own self and their own self-interests, doing what they want to do with their lives. Or do they decide to fully surrender every part of their life over to the Lord and go with His divine plan for their lives rather than their own.

If you decide to follow and serve the Lord, then God will call you and you will then have to take that big leap off the edge of the cliff in order to learn how to fly into the calling that He has placed on your life.

Many Christians have missed out on their true callings from the Lord because they did not have enough faith and belief in Him and to fully trust on the Holy Spirit.

Just think how much more good fruits we could produce, and how much more we could accomplish for the Lord if we could all learn how to be really led by the Holy Spirit on a daily basis, and how to really walk with His power and anointing flowing through us.

Eagles are also considered master fisherman. They are very good in locking in on their prey and then swooping down to catch them.

How many times have you seen videos where an eagle will swoop down on a body of water and pick up a fish swimming near the surface with perfect accuracy, and catching them on the very first attempt? They are

absolute masters at hunting down and catching their prey, whether that prey is on land or in the water.

Just as eagles are considered to be master fisherman by how they can catch fish in water – we, as Christians, have been called by the Lord to be **"fishers of men,"** just like Jesus and the apostles were in the beginning of the New Testament.

Our number one job in this life is to try and get as many people saved as we possibly can. Personal evangelism within our own circle of influence is something that each and every Christian can do for the Lord, and it is something that we should always keep our radars up for – as you never know when the Holy Spirit will move on you to lead you to someone He will want you to witness to, whether it be someone you might know or a complete total stranger.

Though eagles will mate for life, for the most part you will always see them flying alone in the skies.

As Christians, we are all part of the body of Christ, where the little finger is just as important as the big toe. However, the Bible also tells us that many are called but few are chosen. I believe this verse is referring to our calls in the Lord, not to our personal salvation in Him.

What this verse is telling us is that many of the people that God is calling are not being chosen for various reasons. What this means is that at times you may feel totally alone, depending on the type of calling that God has placed on your life and exactly where you are at in the point of development of that calling.

Witchcraft in the Church

David was alone when he took on Goliath. No one else would step on the battlefield with him when he took on that evil blasphemous giant. Peter was alone when he stepped out of the boat to walk on water, as the Bible says that the rest of the apostles were too scared to try and do it on their own. Moses was all by himself for 40 years in the backside of the desert before God called him out to deliver the Israelites from Egypt. David was hiding out in caves from Saul for quite a number of years before he was finally called out to become the greatest king of Israel.

At times, you may feel totally isolated and alone at the spot where God may have you at. When you are in these kinds of dry times and seasons with the Lord, just keep pressing forward and flying alone like the eagle does – and sooner or later God will bring you forth into the heart of your call where everyone will then see you and even work with you on the call that God has placed on your life.

For the most part, eagles will always be found living on some type of higher ground. As Christians, we are already living on higher ground as compared to the rest of the world as a result of who we are in Christ.

We are now born again children of the Most High God. We are now kings and priests of the Lord. We now have the Holy Spirit, along with His power and knowledge residing on the inside of us to help lead us, sanctify us, and empower us so we can all be used by the Lord in a mighty way for ministry.

This is why the Lord is calling all of us to stay in the world, but not to be an actual part of the world. In other words, we are to be in the world, but not of the world. We are to keep ourselves separate from the corruption, pollution, vices, and sins of this world so God can keep us on His straight and narrow road for the rest of our earthly lives.

We live on this higher ground as a result of our position in Jesus. And we always need to keep reminding ourselves that we are living on this higher ground, as the world will always do everything it can to try and drag us down into their lower way of living.

Another very powerful trait of the eagle is that they are very bold, courageous, and powerful. Eagles have literally been seen engaging with poisonous snakes and tearing their heads off with their beak. They have been seen going right through major storm clouds, where most birds will fly away and hide in safety until the storm has passed.

As we have stated numerous times in some of the articles in our spiritual warfare section, God is calling all of us to become good and mighty soldiers of Jesus Christ. He is asking all of us to put on His armor and to engage with demons and to cast them out of people when necessary.

Just like the eagle has no fear of any man, beast, or snake – in the same way we should have no fear of any demonic spirit or any evil human being since we all have God Himself totally on our side. The Bible tells us that greater is He that is in us than he who is in the world. David perfectly proved that point when he took out Goliath with one perfectly, well-placed blow.

Witchcraft in the Church

Just like the eagle is the most powerful and feared bird in the sky – in the same way God the Father can personally raise you up to be a mighty and courageous soldier for Him so you can do great and mighty exploits in the calling that He has personally placed on your life.

Due to the way eagles look and act, many people consider them almost majestic and invincible. They seem to have a look of royalty about them.

We as born again Christians, have this same air of royalty about us since we are now considered kings and priests of the Lord due to the sacrifice that Jesus has personally made for all of us with His death on the cross.

This majestic royalty that we now have operating through us all comes direct from Jesus. It does not come directly from us, or any of the good works that we may have done to-date for the Lord. It all comes to us as a direct result of Jesus dying on the cross for all of our sins.

Only the blood that Jesus has personally shed for each one of us on the cross is what makes us kings and priests before Him, lest we all get puffed up with our own pride and arrogance, thinking this was all of our own doing and making.

Once eagles mate with their partners, they will stay true and loyal to that other eagle for life. In the same way, once God leads us to the mate that He will want us to marry in this life, He will expect us to stay true, loyal, and faithful to that mate literally to the day we die.

Hélèné Fulton

In this day and age, where 70% of all marriages are still failing and ending up in divorce, this is a tall order for many to stay faithful to their spouses. God hates adultery and it is time for you to repent and turn back to God. There are only two accounts were God will allow a divorce. I discuss this further in this book.

God expects all of us to honour our vows and commitments made at the wedding altar. God takes marriage and the vows that come with it very, very seriously, and it is nothing to be trifled with or taken for granted once you hit a few minor speed bumps in the marriage.

The Holy Spirit is the Helper and Counsellor, and He can help heal any hurts or misgivings that may have occurred in the marriage if you will just learn how to open yourself up to Him and allow Him to work in whatever state your marriage may be in.

Another very interesting quality that eagles have is that they are very patient. Documentary film crews have filmed eagles spotting rabbits they will target as prey. Once the rabbit senses the danger, he will then go hiding in a hole, sometimes for as long as an hour or two before he finally comes back out.

The eagle will then wait for that hour or two until the rabbit finally comes back out again. And once he does, the eagle will then swoop down and catch him within seconds. As a result of his patience, the eagle will then be rewarded with a big fat meal.

In the same way, we all need the patience of the eagle, especially in the type of world we now live in with every thing being done at breakneck speed and people's fuses being shortened as a result of all of the high stress that we are forced to live under.

This is why one of the 9 fruits of the Holy Spirit is the fruit of patience, as we all need His patience operating through us so we can weather the storm clouds of this turbulent life.

Another very fascinating quality that eagles have is that they have two sets of eyes. The first set is their natural eye which they have when they are in a resting mode.

However, when they start to take flight on these strong wind thermals, they have a second eye that comes in on them. This second eye then enables them to fly on these strong wind thermals without damaging their original eye. This second eye is also used when they are seen flying through actual storm clouds. The heavy winds from a storm cloud could easily damage their normal natural eye, and this second eye gives them a protective covering as they are navigating through these heavy storm clouds.

As Christians, we also have two sets of eyes operating in us. The first set is our normal natural eye which we use to see the natural world in which we live in. However, we also have a second set of eyes and that is the eyes of the Holy Spirit.

Since we all have the Holy Spirit living on the inside of us, we also have His eyes available to us at times to see things from His perspective. As you start to draw closer to the Lord in your own personal relationship with Him, there will be times that He will allow you to **"see"** things as He sees them. You will start **"seeing"** what certain Scripture verses may mean. You will start to **"see"** what the real truth is in many of the matters of your own personal life.

When this starts to occur, this is the Holy Spirit Himself allowing you to see things through His eyes, not your eye. This is highly supernatural event when it starts to occur. It is God Himself literally allowing you to see things from His point of view and perspective.

The Bible says that the truth will set you free. But you first have to see what that truth is before it can start to set you free. This is why we all need the eyes of the Holy Spirit operating in us, so we can start to see what the real truth is on many of the different matters and issues in our own personal lives.

Just like the eagle needs his two sets of eyes in order to be able to live and survive in this world, in the same way we need both our natural eyes and the eyes of the Holy Spirit operating in us so we can properly work and function for the Lord in this life.

When baby eagles are first born, the mother eagle will build the nest in which to raise up her new-borns in the wilderness, away from mainstream society. This is done so she can safely raise them up without any type of harm coming to them.

In the same way, the Lord will sometimes build up His eagles in a wilderness type setting. Again, Moses was in the backside of the desert for 40 years before God called him out to complete the greatest deliverance mission of all time. David was in the caves of the wilderness for a number of years, possibly for 13-15 years, before he was called out by God to become the greatest king that Israel has ever had.

Some of you who are reading this right now may be in your wilderness setting with the Lord, where He is slowly raising you up in your calling for Him. It is sometimes in these wilderness type settings that your greatest strides in spiritual growth are actually made in Him.

Many of the creatures God has created have colour patterns that blend in with their natural surroundings so as to protect them from other predators. However, not so with the eagle. The American bald eagle has dark brown skin with a white colour head. As a result of this contrasting colour pattern, they can easily be seen from quite a distance.

I know this may be stretching this analogy a bit, but I believe that the dark skin of the eagle lines up with our flesh coloured skins, and the white colour on the head and face of the eagle line up with the presence and power of the Holy Spirit living in us. In other words, it is symbolic of the anointing that we have operating in us through the Holy Spirit.

People who walk with a very strong anointing from the Lord are very noticeable from a distance. You can "see" the anointing of God all over them. You can "see" the manifest presence of the Holy Spirit in the form of a transparent glow radiating out of their faces. These people have developed very strong personal relationships with the Lord over a number of years and they are walking very close with Him in working out their own personal calls for Him in this life.

Just like the eagle stands out in his environment as a result of his might, prowess, and contrasting color pattern in the animal kingdom – in the same way, highly anointed Christians also stand out in their surroundings due to the presence and power of God Almighty Himself radiating out of them.

Jesus Himself has told us in His Word that He is our light, and that once we have His light shining through us, that we are not to try and hide it underneath the table. We are to let His light shine through us so we can reach the rest of the world with His message of eternal salvation.

Once you isolate all of the main qualities of the eagle, I do not think it is a coincidence that they all perfectly line up with what God would like to have worked into each one of us. I believe when God says in the above verse from Isaiah that we will mount up with wings **like eagles,** He is meaning exactly what He is saying in this verse.

Once again, here are the main attributes and qualities of the mighty eagle, the most powerful and feared bird in the skies:

1. Master fliers
2. Master fishermen
3. Fly alone
4. Live on higher ground
5. Extremely bold, courageous, and powerful
6. Majestic
7. Mate for life

Witchcraft in the Church

8. Very patient
9. Have two sets of eyes
10. Nests are built in the wilderness
11. Noticeable from a distance as a result of contrasting colour patterns

I believe the Lord is in the process of rising up an army of mighty eagles. I believe we are living in the last days as prophesied in the Bible, and God will be launching this army of eagles onto the earth in an effort to get as many people saved and on that [2]rapture train as He possibly can before the end finally comes.

Some of you who are reading this article right now might be one of these eagles being raised up by the Lord. If you are, study this eagle analogy very carefully, as I believe the Lord is giving all of us a very powerful and profound analogy.

---

[2]The Bible speaks about being caught up as per the verse below.

[15] According to the Lord's word, we tell you that we who are still alive, who are left until the coming of the Lord, will certainly not precede those who have fallen asleep. [16] For the Lord himself will come down from heaven, with a loud command, with the voice of the archangel and with the trumpet call of God, and the dead in Christ will rise first. [17] After that, we who are still alive and are left will be **caught up** together with them in the clouds to meet the Lord in the air. And so we will be with the Lord forever.

1 Thessalonians 4:15-17

Hélèné Fulton

Chapter 5: Encounter with a witch

3 June 2011

On the 3rd of June I had a photo vision. It looked like an old photo, yellow in color, resembling old photos. However, the photo was alive with beings that resembled worms that where sitting on drums while they were smoking cigarettes.

Interpretation

God was showing me that the dark kingdom was robbing me of my prosperity.

The drums represent my prosperity. The worm like beings on the drums smoking were demons.

Action Taken

In the name of Jesus Christ I cancelled and rebuked the demons that were stealing my prosperity, I then asked Father God to command Satan to give back all of my stolen blessings, 7 fold, in the name of Jesus Christ.

God also showed another person how Jacob's father went to a [3]Sangoma. He paid the Sangoma a roll of money and they did a ritual where they took mice and cut them open and put the inside of a mattress and cotton wool inside of the mice. They then said some chants and spells in order to steal Jacob and my prosperity.

This was also canceled with a similar prayer as the one above.

---

[3] A Sangoma is a Witch usually a black person can be male or female.

3 June 2011

That night I had a dream where [4]Kenny Vaaltyn, a colored man and a dear brother to me in Christ, was on a big stage presenting his music ministry. At this time Kenny was unknown and was just praying for a breakthrough with his music.

Interpretation

Sometimes God will show you the things to come in a dream or in a vision.
Around October 2012 Kenny was offered a contract to produce his 1st CD at the age of 62. Kenny is travelling South Africa over weekends and is now preaching and singing at various churches in South Africa.

5 June 2011

I was lying on my bed thinking of all the miracles that happened during the Healing & Deliverance Crusade and I got a black and white photo vision. The photo transpired like a movie.

I was at a big intersection; the traffic light was out of order. In the right-hand lane, which incidentally is supposed to be the fast lane, large trucks were blocking my view.

---

[4] Real name. If you want to order Kenny's CD it is available through our ministry.

Hélèné Fulton

Pedestrians where crossing as I was about to cross the traffic light. 3 People that were crossing stood out from the crowd in front of them and behind them. One of them was wearing a dress. I noticed that I could not see their feet and it looked like they were floating as they did not touch the ground and they had a shining silhouette around them. All 3 of them, those who stood out from the rest, looked directly at me when they were crossing the intersection.

I sat up and immediately wrote down this vision in my notebook.

As I lay back I smelled a strong odor of sulphur. I asked Jacob whether he could smell it too, he said that he couldn't.

Interpretation

Since danger was approaching me, God send 3 angels to protect me.

The 3 pedestrians that crossed the road were angles in human form. The smell of sulphur that followed was the odor of the defeated demons that were defeated in the physical realm by the 3 angels.

During this time Light the World Ministries had a Healing & Deliverance crusade which was supposed to last for one weekend only, but due to an overwhelming spate of interest it turned out to run for more than 2 weeks. We had scheduled private sessions with families and individuals as we are aware that people do not want others to hear about the mistakes they made in the past. Here, I would like to share certain things that happened during this time. Even how a Pastor's unbelief can hinder his parishioners' path to progress, and also delay, or even completely stop their blessings.

During this time 5 people were given new hearts by the Lord. I saw how the Lord placed a new physical heart into the 4 men and 1 lady. Every time after the healing the person would tell me that they have medical records on how bad their heart was and that they were waiting on a heart transplant or operation.

God revealed the name of a person who had been given a bracelet with a curse on it and we requested to see this person as the person was not in the church but her name was given while busy ministering to one of her family members. The curse was broken as the bracelet was burned.

Cursed objects needs to burn to sometimes break the curse. By giving it to another person or throwing it away does not break the curse on it.

God reveled how He send His angels to protect one of His children the previous night from an accident that was planned to kill her because she started to fulfill her calling. Angels basically picked up her car and put it on the side just in time from an oncoming truck that would have flattened her car. I was busy ministering to the person when I had the vision of the accident. It was so real that I even covered my face as it felt as if I was in the car and the truck was going to crush me to. When I explained to the person what I saw, she confirmed that this is what actually happened to her the previous night. She said that she had no idea how she got to the other side of the road as she just closed her eyes and prayed.

God also showed us a young man who was in an accident at a very young age and it looked like he was the driver of the vehicle and he took the shoes of one of his dead friends and just by putting on those shoes he brought all that friends demons and curses onto himself. Now this young man was not in line with God that is why Satan had the legal right to do this to him. He also lied to authorities and to his parents on details about this accident.

It is with sadness that I also need to inform you that even though God saved that woman from a definite death in the accident. Four months later she was not willing to help this ministry as she rather wanted to side with an out of line pastor Koos who also prevented others from getting their blessings as he promised her that she can preach in his church.

This young man was told to do a specific task but due to pastor Koos telling him otherwise all the demons came back and brought some new demons with them. I was told by a reliable source that this young man is now using drugs.

Never ever sell your soul to the devil! More on this pastor later in the book.

What are legal rights?

A legal right is something that can give demons an opportunity to enter or torment you, or gives demons the right to remain in you even when you try to cast them out. Some of the most common legal rights that I faced when ministering to people are:

Sins (especially wilful sins): When you commit sin, it gives the enemy a legal right to affect you in one way or another. The bigger the sin, the bigger the door that is opened to the devil. Unholy thoughts entering your mind can open the door to a demon of lust, which eventually causes the person to commit adultery.

It starts when we are tempted to think the wrong thing, then when we accept it and make it a habit, it opens the door for the enemy to move in further. Behind the bad habit that is formed, lies a demonic compulsion that isn't easily resisted. Continuing down this path, opens more doors to the enemy, and eventually that person will find himself committing rape, etc. because the feelings and desires the demons push on that person are irresistible. Once committing those sins, even bigger doors are then opened, and the problem is like a snowball going down the hill.

Sin opens the door to demons, which push us in the direction to more sins, which open you, wider to more demons.

How do you fix it? Repent! Verbally confess and repent of your sins that have given the enemy legal rights in your life.

If we confess our sins, He is faithful and just to forgive us our sins and to cleanse us from all unrighteousness.
1 John 1:9

Soul ties: Some of the most popular and destructive soul ties are formed during adultery or fornication.

Héléné Fulton

Or do you not know that he who is joined to a harlot is one body *with her?* For "the two," He says, "shall become one flesh."

1 Corinthians 6:16

The above Bible verse warns us not to have sexual relations with a prostitute because we become one flesh (flesh as in soul realm kind of flesh, not a physical flesh) with that person.

This ungodly soul tie is like a rope between two persons that demons can use to their advantage to cross from one person to another. If that person had demons tormenting them, and you had sex with them, it unites the two persons, and therefore a soul tie is created, and the demons tormenting that person can also have rights to torment you.

Sex within a marriage does not create unhealthy soul ties as the Bible says that the marriage bed is un-defiled. To create an evil soul tie you would need defilement.

How do you fix it? Repent! Then break the soul ties by saying this out loud.

"I now renounce, break and sever all unholy soul ties created between myself and _____ through the act of adultery in Jesus' name!"

Soul ties can also be formed between yourself and another person, without any sexual relationship. Other soul ties can be created through unhealthy relationships, such as being so close to a parent that you take their advice over God's advice. Again, repentance and the breaking of the soul ties in Jesus' name is the way to go about solving this problem.

Things that could hold back the breaking of a soul tie, is a physical object given to you from the other person, through a sinful relationship. If you were given a ring, or bra or a love gift through an adulterous relationship, for example, then those gift(s) can hold the soul tie together. If the gift is valuable, and not necessarily bad in itself, then it's best to sell the gift. If the gift is demonic or unholy, then it's best to burn the gift.

Demonic vows: A demonic vow can be like a spiritual signature that the enemy uses as a legal right to gain access into our lives. Demonic vows can be made consciously or unconsciously. Often when a person joins a cult coven (a group of witches), they are required to make vows with the devil. Demonic vows can be made unconsciously just by dabbling with the occult. Just by getting curious about the occult and reading forbidden materials (including horoscopes) can give the enemy your spiritual signature; it tells the enemy that you're interested. Jesus warns us not to make any vows at all. The only vows I can see are practical and good are those made during a marriage ceremony.

If you have made vows that do not glorify God, then you should repent and renounce those vows verbally and seek God's forgiveness. Do this verbally; because vows are made verbally, breaking them is also done verbally.

Un-forgiveness: When we don't forgive others, God won't forgive us. When God doesn't forgive us, it leaves our sins remaining, which can give the enemy legal rights into our lives.

Therefore the kingdom of heaven is like a certain king who wanted to settle accounts with his servants.[24] And when he had begun to settle accounts, one was brought to him who owed him ten thousand talents.[25] But as he was not able to pay, his master commanded that he be sold, with his wife and children and all that he had, and that payment be made. [26] The servant therefore fell down before him, saying, 'Master, have patience with me, and I will pay you all.' [27] Then the master of that servant was moved with compassion, released him, and forgave him the debt.

[28] "But that servant went out and found one of his fellow servants who owed him a hundred denarii; and he laid hands on him and took *him* by the throat, saying, 'Pay me what you owe!' [29] So his fellow servant fell down at his feet and begged him, saying, 'Have patience with me, and I will pay you all.' [30] And he would not, but went and threw him into prison till he should pay the debt. [31] So when his fellow servants saw what had been done, they were very grieved, and came and told their master all that had been done. [32] Then his master, after he had called him, said to him, 'You wicked servant! I forgave you all that debt because you begged me. [33] Should you not also have had compassion on your fellow servant, just as I had pity on you?' [34] And his master was angry, and delivered him to the torturers until he should pay all that was due to him.

[35] "So My heavenly Father also will do to you if each of you, from his heart, does not forgive his brother his trespasses."

Matthew 18:23-35

Keep in mind that the tormenters this scripture is referring to are demons. The legal ground the enemy may be standing on to torment you may very well be rooted in un-forgiveness! I've heard that the single most common reason that people aren't healed is because they are holding un-forgiveness in their hearts, and I believe it! Forgiveness is not an option; it's a necessity!

Repent for holding bitterness in your heart against others, and make a solid choice to forgive those who have wronged you (also confirm your choice by verbally forgiving them in front of God as it is not always possible to be in front of that person), and release the bitterness and hurt from your heart against them.

Witchcraft in the Church

Ancestral sins: When you involve yourself in the deeper sins or the occult world, you not only open demonic doors in your own life, but also in the lives of your children and grandchildren.

you shall not bow down to them nor serve them. For I, the LORD your God, *am* a jealous God, visiting the iniquity of the fathers upon the children to the third and fourth *generations* of those who hate Me,

Exodus 20:5

If your ancestors have committed sins or have been involved in the occult, then it's a good idea to confess those sins, to the best of your ability to God, and ask Him for forgiveness. Please also take note that if someone in your family committed suicide you also need to add this.

But if they confess their iniquity and the iniquity of their fathers, with their unfaithfulness in which they were unfaithful to Me, and that they also have walked contrary to Me,
⁴¹ and *that* I also have walked contrary to them and have brought them into the land of their enemies;
if their uncircumcised hearts are humbled, and they accept their guilt—
⁴² then I will remember My covenant with Jacob, and My covenant with Isaac and My covenant with Abraham I will remember;
I will remember the land.

Leviticus 26:40-42

Even though you personally aren't guilty of those sins, they may have caused curses in your life, and those curses need to be broken. Common ways to tell if ancestral sins are involved is if your siblings or ancestors have experienced or are experiencing the same or similar problem that you are.

The legal grounds have already been broken! If any spirits are remaining, they must be cast out.

Childhood rejection: Much demonic bondage is caused during childhood. For example, if a parent shows rejection toward their child, a spirit of rejection may enter.

If you have been rejected by either your parents or somebody else, you must make a solid choice to forgive that person(s), and release the hurt in your heart against them. The spirit of rejection is usually present in these situations, and should be renounced.

Points of weakness: When the person experiences weakness, such as emotional shock, physical trauma, fearful experiences during childhood, and other areas to which the natural walls of defence in the physical, spiritual or emotional system of a person are weakened, it leaves us vulnerable for the enemy to attach himself to us. The same is true with drinking excessive amounts of alcohol, and especially true with drugs, because they lower our defences, and since demons thrive on weakness, they love to move right in and setup camp.

If there was any bitterness involved (say somebody caused the traumatic experience for you, and you are still holding it against them), then you must forgive the person who hurt you, and repent for harbouring bitterness in your heart against them. If the point of weakness was caused by your own sin, such as drinking or drugs, then confess and repent of that sin. If the demons entered solely through traumatic experience, and none of it was anybody's fault, then the demons are 100% trespassers in this situation, and need to be told to leave!

Spoken self-curses: The words we say have spiritual value, the Bible says to bless and not curse, and that the tongue has the power of life and death. If you walk around saying, "I wish I could just die," a demon may hear you and can go to God and say, "Look, she wants to die!" and here comes a spirit of death.

Jacob's parents use to tell my children that they are useless and I had to renounce this every time.

Take back what you spoke against yourself, renounce it! Repent for speaking such thing(s), and break the curse(s) in Jesus' name!

Cursed objects: Physical objects can carry spiritual value, such as idols, occult books, rings, movies, charms, etc. If you brought any Indian or pagan religion artefact's into your home, you could be opening the door for demons to enter and bother the people within your home. Land can also become defiled by the sins of its owners

(for all these abominations the men of the land have done, who *were* before you, and thus the land is defiled),
Leviticus 18:27

Burn, destroy or get rid of any physical objects that you have that could be cursed.

But the idols He shall utterly abolish.
Isaiah 2:18

Hélèné Fulton

It is Biblical to burn cursed objects. Repent for bringing such objects into your home if you are responsible for them! Land can be cleansed by prayer and repenting of the sins of the previous owners.

Renounce demons: Renounce any known demons that have been invited in (i.e. spirit guides), and any interest or involvement in the occult or Satanism. Also renounce any demons that you know need to be cast out. This helps let the demons know that you are no longer interested in having them around.

Other helpful things to look for: When did the bondage start? Try to pinpoint how the problem started and what gave the demons the ability to enter. Look for any involvement in the occult, sins, vows, traumatic experiences, etc. along with any unusual happenings emotionally, spiritually or mentally.

A lady who could not walk for more than 20 years was set free from bondage left the church on her feet, walking upright.

Here is her story: This lady had a fight with her daughter-in-law. Then after they said that they were both sorry for the fight the daughter-in-law borrowed red shoes from the mother-in-law. After returning the red shoes – the moment this mother-in-law put the shoes on her own feet she found herself unable to walk, even after removing the shoes she was unable to walk. As time transpired, it became worse until she could no longer walk at all anymore! This curse even transferred to her torso, her upper body which was beginning to show signs of weakness. The evening of this lady's healing and deliverance she had to be assisted by two children and she used crutches.

Witchcraft in the Church

We removed the crutches and I was holding her with my hands around her waist. I remember praying softly to Father God not to let the lady fall as she felt like jelly and I had to hold on for dear life.

Now while embracing this lady I determined something which felt like a thick padlock around her waist. What was done in secret was that the daughter-in-law took this pair of red shoes to a traditional doctor (Sangoma), or in fact, a witch doctor that placed a curse on the wearer of the shoes. This curse entailed the placing of a padlock around the waist of the wearer of the shoes, who was in fact the owner of the shoes.

After praying for this woman, she fell under the power. When she came back she at first did not know where she was but she stood up by herself and then walked to where her kids were seated.

On the same night a women whose one leg was shorter than the other was touched by God and healed completely. Her shorter leg grew to the same length as the other.

Several people with back injuries were healed and their backs were restored.

One man lost a couple of million Rands due to the fact that he signed a contract with someone with whom he placed complete trust in. This man wanted to commit suicide when he thought that he had lost all he had worked for his entire life, however God restored him.

Hélèné Fulton

There are nonetheless many warnings about who we are to place our trust in.

Do not put your trust in princes, *nor* in a son of man, in whom *there is* no help.

Psalm 146:3

The God of my strength, in whom I will trust; my shield and the horn of my salvation,
My stronghold and my refuge; my Savior, You save me from violence.

2 Samuel 22:3

During this time I also had encounters with 2 witches. These were white women in their 50's that were practicing witchcraft, both also very prominent women inside this church.

My encounter with Hester the witch

A certain woman whose name was Hester was forever coming to my office saying all the right things, for instance, she loved to quote the following Bible verse:

You are of God, little children, and have overcome them, **because He who is in you is greater than he who is in the world.**

1 John 4:4

Hester also told me her story. She grew up in a home where she was abused by several men. All were family members and very close friends of the family. Her entire family was witches and warlocks. As a young girl, from the age of 9 some of the men would have sex with her as part of their rituals; this would include anal sex since this is the preferred way of the demons. Some of the men also like to

Witchcraft in the Church

[5]Defecateon her after they had their way with her. This is a sign of the utter disregard they had for her dignity as a human being!

She also married a Satanist later, out of this marriage 4 children were born, of which the youngest was a son of 19 years; this was when I first met Hester. Hester led us to believe that it was her wish to receive deliverance and to accept Jesus Christ. However, this was a lie from the pit of Hades since she had no true wish to truly accept Jesus Christ as her Lord and Saviour.

Hester's son, the boy of 19 confessed to me that his parents wanted to sacrifice him by fire to their god Satan. They built a pyre of old motor car tires on which they placed him and set it alight! However, another family member extinguished the fire.

Hester exchanges her youngest son's mental ability for her "powers" which result in her perfectly once normal son now being mentally slow for his age.

I had a beautiful garden in front of my office. After Hester came to visit me every day in my office I noticed that my flowers unexpectedly sprouted lice that were totally resistant to any form of treatment. Hester's one daughter worked for me as a secretary at this time. When she started working for me I had no idea what her mother was practicing. She mentioned to me that she had all sorts of insects in her house and that it has even gone

---

[5]**Defecation** (colloquially known as a **bowel movement** or **bm**) is the final act of digestion, by which organisms eliminate solid, semisolid, or liquid waste material (feces) from the digestive tract via the anus.

into the mattresses and clothes. She said that she has run out of ideas of how to get rid of these insects.

Hester lived with this daughter of hers, and the church ceremony that we held, for the healing and deliverance crusade was providing food for this tiny family.

The gift of the Spirit of God that was necessary at that time was discernment; God the Holy Spirit graciously granted me access to this in this instance with Hester. It became clear to me that Hester was a witch; apparently there is such a thing as white and black witchcraft and witches; however there are no witches in Christianity, no witch, black or white can possibly serve God, since Satan is father of anything ungodly. It became as clear as daylight to me that Hester did not want to accept Christ Jesus into her life, it was merely an attempt to throw us, the workers of God off track . . . her lord and master was none other than Satan himself.

God through His Spirit gave me this portion of Scripture:

"You shall not permit a sorceress to live.
Exodus 22:18

Now do not get me wrong and go and put all witches to death, tie them up and place them on the stake. It was clearly evident that this is not what God wanted.
God told me to break all ties and links with Hester, including her entire family. I immediately did as prompted by the Holy Spirit.

After I broke all ties with Hester and her family my garden was restored right away and all insects were gone the next morning, vanished into thin air, isn't our God Awesome! However, this was not as easy as it seems. I received threats and rude text messages from Hester for many weeks after this.

She would even text message the Pastor of the church [6] we were working through at the time, telling him that it is his responsibility to keep her and her daughter fed. God showed me that she was chanting over the food and robbing the person who provided the food of his prosperity. This is the character of Satan:

The thief does not come except to steal, and to kill, and to destroy. I have come that they may have life, and that they may have *it* more abundantly.

John 10:10

One of Hester's text messages read: "you, jesus christ of Nazareth, watch out my lord is bigger and stronger than you."

Now, please take note that I have phrased it in the exact same way as Hester texted me. She was so conditioned and brainwashed by Satan that she thought he (Satan) is the lord over and above Jesus Christ.

It was during this time that God started teaching me that whatever you give, whether it is food or old clothes or even new clothes or a tip, always wash it with the blood of Jesus Christ. When you do this Satan and his workers cannot use it against you and they will not be able to use it in the spiritual realm either.

---

[6] My ministry team and I

I started implementing this method even when I went for normal, everyday shopping.

It is essential that we as born again Christians realize that with so many Muslim and Hindu owned shops we have no idea what the owners of these shops do with the money that we have paid for our purchases.

In fact this habit has become lifestyle. It is a lifestyle in which I protect my money and the possessions I receive from sponsors from this day forward.

I've learned that a butcher bought R3000 worth of groceries for Hester and even though I did tell this person to cover the groceries with the blood of Jesus Christ. He told me he does not believe in these things that foolish Christians cling to since he deems them to be irrational. Now, see how our God works in righteousness. A month later the butchery was bankrupt and he had to close his doors for business. It is now 3 years later and this man is still unemployed and has lost everything that he built up over years.

About a year later I learned that the pastor from the church told this man that I am crazy and he should not believe what I tell him. Well, God said to me that many people will persecute me but I should not let this worry me or upset me as many people will be helped through Light the World Ministries (www.lighttheworldministries.co.za), Deliverance Ministry (www.deliveranceministry.co.za & Prayer Academy (www.prayeracademy.co.za).

My encounter with Cornelia the witch

Cornelia was also a prominent congregation member in the same church as Hester. In fact besides Hester and Cornelia

Witchcraft in the Church

this church with about 60 church members had 3 witches and 2 warlocks (male witch) in the congregation.

Although God told me 6 times before this that I am His prophet through various methods, I had to hear it from a witch the 7th time before I started to use the title. Now, even though I did not use the title of prophet, it took nothing away from the fact that I was a prophet ordained by Christ Jesus Himself. It also did not hold back the spiritual and physical attacks as everything always happens in the spiritual realm before it manifests in the physical.

On this particular Sunday Jacob and I went to church and he wore his New Apostolic outfit, like I used to call it. Jacob and his parents and grant parents come from an Old Apostolic background. His grandfather was a priest in the New Apostolic church. His New Apostolic outfit was a Black suit, white shirt and black tie. A must for men in the Old and New Apostolic church. More information on false religions and cults in my book on False Religions.

Please note that Light the World Ministries are following the doctrine of Christ.

Whoever transgresses and does not abide in the doctrine of Christ does not have God. He who abides in the doctrine of Christ has both the Father and the Son.
2 John 1:9

We were standing by the door chatting to other congregation members and Cornelia walked in. She hugged my ex-husband, Jacob, as if they knew each other and then she said something that I did not comprehend until much later that day.

She said to me that it is so difficult to be a Prophetess being a woman in a man's world, and then she pointed at me saying, "As you should know." Cornelia subsequently made an appointment with me to come for deliverance; she was accompanied by the Pastor's wife from this very same church. During deliverance Cornelia told me how her husband forced her to have sex with his friends, both normal sex and [7]anal sex. They also partook in bestiality, this is when man partakes in sexual acts with animals, and this is taking an upright stance against God. Cornelia has had 2 strokes and according to her, her mother-in-law has also had two strokes causing their left leg and arm to be numb and slow to move, or react. Further Symptoms include spasticity which is stiff or inflexible muscles with overstated, deep tendon impulses (i.e., a sudden involuntary swiping of the arm reflex, sometimes the leg may involuntary tremble, or quiver). The condition may very well interfere with normal walking, general movement, or even speech.

God the Holy Spirit once again released on me the spirit of discernment which indicated to me that Cornelia is actually higher up in the coven[8] than Hester and that they "fly together" at night.

Cornelia refused to say the salvation prayer and accept Jesus Christ as her Lord and Savior that day. I clearly recall that this happened on a Thursday. I did not think Cornelia

---

[7] Anal sex is very demonic

[8] **Coven:**
"a gathering of witches," 1662, earlier (c.1500) a variant of covent, cuvent early forms of convent (q.v.)
"Letters on Demonology and Witchcraft" (1830). Dictionary.com

Witchcraft in the Church

would ever show up at the same church since she was exposed in front of the Pastor's wife, but that very Sunday evening as I attended a sermon preached by a friend and colleague preach a sermon on protecting your money and possessions with the blood of Jesus Christ, Cornelia showed up 5 minutes into the sermon. I recall that everyone sat on the left side of the church that evening. Cornelia and one other member, Ernest sat on their lonesome on the right hand side, at the back of the church.

During the sermon as it was explained that Satan will even send a person that one will really pity, being deformed, disabled, handicapped, mentally or physically, sometimes even cripple standing at the traffic light begging for money, or a presumably single mother with a child. One must be very vigilant as they could be "agents" working for the Dark Kingdom collecting money for the Antichrist. It was also explained that R5 equals R500 000 in the spiritual world and how they can drain your funds just by you donating money to them without protecting it first with the blood of Jesus Christ. This is an extremely helpful and safe habit one should develop into a lifestyle.

It was just after this was said that Cornelia manifested in church. Here is what happened. The entire congregation started smelling an odor of burning. It smelled strongly of sulphur. It was so strong that Ernest ran outside as he thought something is burning outside. Jacob went outside with Ernest and I was told later by my son-in-law that Jacob told Ernest that it was the smell of sulphur. God told me later that evening that this is why He gave me the following Bible verse as part of the ministry. This was God's words to me, "My child my people are being misled by the Pastors and the Pastors today are not telling my people the truth because they are too worried about the tithe and offering, therefore money means more to my Pastors than My Word.

My people are destroyed for lack of knowledge. Because you have rejected knowledge, I also will reject you from being priest for Me; because you have forgotten the law of your God, I also will forget your children.

Hosea 4:6

Therefore my people have gone into captivity, because *they have* no knowledge; their honorable men *are* famished, and their multitude dried up with thirst.

Isaiah 5:13`

Please note: If you have anal sex, with any one even with your own husband it is demonic. Repent from this immediately and ask God for forgiveness for this sin.

If you are involved in sex orgies or any type of [9]swingers, repent as this is how Satan ends his meetings with his followers.

Any type of sexual activity other than with your husband or wife is wrong in God's eyes.

---

[9] **Swinging** or (rarely) **partner swapping** is a non-monogamous behavior, in which singles or partners in a committed relationship engage in sexual activities with others as a recreational or social activity.[1] Swinging can take place in a number of contexts, ranging from spontaneous sexual activity at informal gatherings of friends to planned regular social meetings to "hooking up" with like-minded people at a swingers' club.

Witchcraft in the Church

Chapter 6: Gifts of the Spirit

But the manifestation of the Spirit is given to each one for the profit of all: 8 for to one is given the word of wisdom through the Spirit, to another the word of knowledge through the same Spirit, 9 to another faith by the same Spirit, to another gifts of healings by the same[a] Spirit, 10 to another the working of miracles, to another prophecy, to another discerning of spirits, to another different kinds of tongues, to another the interpretation of tongues. 11 But one and the same Spirit works all these things, distributing to each one individually as He wills.

1 Corinthians 12:7-11

- The Word of Knowledge
- The Word of Wisdom
- The Gift of Prophecy
- The Gift of Faith
- The Gifts of Healings
- The Working of Miracles
- The Discerning of Spirits
- Different Kinds of Tongues
- The Interpretation of Tongues

You will recognise some of these gifts in previous chapters.

The Bible tells us to not only desire spiritual gifts, but to also not be afraid to try and stir these gifts up with the Lord.

Hélèné Fulton

Therefore, brethren, desire earnestly to prophesy, and do not forbid to speak with tongues.

1 Corinthians 14:39

Pursue love, and desire spiritual *gifts,* but especially that you may prophesy.

1 Corinthians 14:1

Do not quench the Spirit.

1 Thessalonians 5:19

Do not neglect the gift that is in you, which was given to you by prophecy with the laying on of the hands of the eldership.

1 Timothy 4:14

Therefore I remind you to stir up the gift of God which is in you through the laying on of my hands.

2 Timothy 1:6

Every believer should ask God for these gifts. Let God know that you are a willing vessel for the manifestations of these gifts, and that you will give Him a full and solid green light to manifest these gifts through you at anytime that He will want to do so.

Remember God is a Gentleman and He will not force Himself on you.

These gifts will be a help and aid to you in your personal walk with the Lord, but will be used to help other people through you.

Let me break down each one of these 9 gifts.

The Word of Knowledge

This gift will manifest the most in your daily life with the Lord. God has perfect knowledge of everything, we don't. You will see how God will impart this knowledge in you when you need it. You will be amazed when this happens. This knowledge is the Holy Spirit giving you specific knowledge on something that you would not have known with your own ability and limited intelligence. This is supernatural knowledge and insight given to you by the Holy Spirit Himself.

Here are some examples

- Solving a problem.
- Finding something that you have misplaced.
- Knowledge on a specific scriptural verse that you need at a specific time.
- How to minister to unsaved people.
- How to handle disputes in your everyday walk with the Lord.
- How to start or run a business.
- Finding the person God wants you to marry.
- Finding the job God wants you to have.
- Knowledge on how to counsel someone through a difficult period in their life.
- Knowledge that God wants to heal someone from an illness.
- Knowledge on what your calling in the Lord is.

The Holy Spirit will work through your human spirit. It is like an inner knowing. It is like a thought that come to mind and you just know that it cannot be from yourself as how would you have known this. I always tell my spiritual children and people that comes for prayers that the very first thought will be the Holy Spirit and you're your flesh and Satan will try and tell you differently. You will suddenly receive a knowing that the Holy Spirit is revealing something to you. This might also come through a vision.

The Word of Wisdom

The Word of Wisdom will work in hand in hand with the word of knowledge. In many cases all you need is a direct word of knowledge from the Holy Spirit to completely solve a problem you are dealing with.

We all need words of wisdom from the Holy Spirit in our daily life, so we will know how to handle different types of problems that occur in our daily lives.

You could receive words of wisdom direct from the Holy Spirit:

- On how to handle your finances to save you from bankruptcy.
- On how to handle a cheating or un-believing spouse.
- How to handle a lawsuit.
- How to handle difficult teenagers or a rude boss or even back stabbing co-workers.

The Gift of Prophecy

The gift of prophecy is when you get a direct message from the Lord to give to someone else. It will be given to you word for word. Always keep a notebook to write these down. Also include the date that you've received it and the name of the person for whom it was meant. Also write down prophecies that are spoken over you.

The Bible tells us that God uses the gift of prophecy to speak edification, exhortation, and comfort to other people.

He who speaks in a [strange] tongue edifies *and* improves himself, but he who prophesies [interpreting the divine will and purpose and teaching with inspiration] edifies *and* improves the church *and* promotes growth [in Christian wisdom, piety, holiness, and happiness

1 Corinthians 14:4 Amplified Bible

Prophecy will also be used to confirm what has already been given to a person previously. God will also confirm what He has already told you earlier so you will know that it really was Him giving you that specific message.

Prophecies from God can cover a wide range of situations. Prophecies could cover everything from predicting future events to counselling or encouraging someone. Prophecy can be confirmation or instructions. Prophecy can also be correction when it is needed.

On 23 July 2012, I prayed in the morning and asked God to give me answers on 12 Questions that I had concerning some pastors and prophets that I knew. I was praying in the spirit, so only God and I knew what I have asked Him. I received a phone call from one of my spiritual daughters at about noon inviting me and some of the other spiritual children to Benny Hinn who was visiting my home town. I did not even know that pastor Hinn was in South Africa.

As we were standing outside one of the men visiting our ministry at the time wanted to say something bad about pastor Hinn. The Holy Spirit immediately prompts me to prevent this man from saying what he was about to. God said to me. That is one of my anointed children.

That evening God answered all 12 of my questions through pastor Benny Hinn's service. What an amazing God.

Prophecy should always line up with Scripture. If not, it should be immediately rejected. God will never go against His own Word when delivering a prophetic word to someone.

Do not quench the Spirit. [20] Do not despise prophecies. [21] Test all things; hold fast what is good.

1 Thessalonians 5:19-21

The Gift of Faith

The gift of faith comes directly from the Holy Spirit.

The Bible tells us that we have a certain measure of faith that has already been given to us by the Lord. Without a certain measure of faith we would not get saved, as the Bible tells us that we are saved by faith through grace. As we continue to draw closer to the Lord in our own personal relationship with Him and as our knowledge increases through the studying of Scripture, so too will our faith increase.

However, there will be times when our own levels of faith in the Lord will not be enough to get the job done that God is expecting us to do. You have been using the gift of healing to heal minor illnesses so your faith is growing but say for instance God wants you to heal through the gift of healing a blind person. Immediately you can sense through your own spirit that your faith is not at that level yet. You don't have the confidence yet to do such a big healing. The Holy Spirit will then manifest His own divine faith into you so that you can now believe and operate on that faith. You will now have the courage to lay hands on that person, and then tell him/her that God is healing his/her eyes.

The Gifts of Healings

One of the things that Jesus wants us to do is to pray for the sick. When we pray for the sick, most of the times they will be healed.

The Holy Spirit can manifest this gift through any believer in order to heal someone. As a result of the Adamic curse that is still in full operation on Earth many people still need healing from all kinds of diseases.

The Holy Spirit can heal you through your own prayers to God through the name of Jesus Christ and He can also use you as His anointed vessel to manifest His healing power through you to help heal someone else.

Both God the Father in the Old Testament and Jesus Christ in the New Testament were healing people. God does not change and He is the same today as He was yesterday and He wants to continue His healing ministry through the Holy Spirit and His anointed believers.

Hélèné Fulton

The Working of Miracles

You will read of many jaw dropping miracles in this book. Believe me I was just as amazed as you are reading it.

Our God is a miracle-working God and He still loves to do them for His people. By studying the Bible you will see that one miracle after another was performed with both God the Father and Jesus Christ.

The Discerning of spirits

The first thing to notice about this gift is that the **"s"** in the word **"spirits"** is with a small **"s."** This means that it is not referring to the Holy Spirit. The only other spirits that are out there that this gift is referring to are the following spirits:

1. **Demonic spirits**

   Demons can literally enter into a person's body if they have legal right to do so. Once they are in someone's body, they will then hide and not show themselves. Demons know if they get caught and exposed they are at risk of that person either finding Jesus if they are not saved yet, or if it is a Christian, that this person will then seek out a deliverance from another believer.

   Since some demons are very good at hiding God needs to activate this gift through some of His own so they can detect when a demon is on the inside of someone and expose its presence. Once the demon has been exposed, then you can set the person up for deliverance.

2. God's angels

From the Bible we learn that God's angels are also spirit beings. God's angels are ministering spirits.

The Bible also warns us that Satan and his demons can appear to us as angels of light. As a result, you will need proper discernment from the Holy Spirit if an angel appears to you.

Beloved, do not believe every spirit, but test the spirits, whether they are of God; because many false prophets have gone out into the world. ² By this you know the Spirit of God: Every spirit that confesses that Jesus Christ has come in the flesh is of God, ³ and every spirit that does not confess that Jesus Christ has come in the flesh is not of God. And this is the *spirit* of the Antichrist, which you have heard was coming, and is now already in the world.
⁴ You are of God, little children, and have overcome them, because He who is in you is greater than he who is in the world.
1 John 4:1-4

3. Human spirits

We are all totally capable of having bad kinds of spirits build up in our systems without the help of any kind of demonic spirits, since we have already been born into this world as corrupt sinners. God will not hesitate to have His Holy Spirit give you major warning signals if you ever start to cross paths with a bad and evil human being who is either targeting you, or any of your close friends or family members for some kind of an evil act.

The Holy Spirit will give you supernatural discernment, insight, and knowledge involving these three kinds of spirits. This gift will be used to expose what is really going on and what spirit is operating within someone.

Different Kinds of Tongues

Tongues is the Holy Spirit giving you the supernatural ability to speak in a foreign tongue that you have no knowledge or ability to speak out on your own.

There are different types of tongues that God will give you through His Spirit. One is a tongue on earth for instance if your language is English, then He can give you the ability to speak in Spanish. Another tongue is directly from heaven, a heavenly language that is not of this earth.

Though I speak with the **tongues of** men and of **angels**, but have not love, I have become sounding brass or a clanging cymbal.
1 Corinthians 13:1

It will be a language that you will not be able to speak out of your own, and only the Holy Spirit's supernatural transmission of this language out of your spirit will give you the ability to be able to speak this language. And whatever tongue the Holy Spirit will give you, you will be able to use it 24/7, whenever you want. It will be your own personal, private, prayer language between you and the Lord.

Singing with the spirit

Therefore let him who speaks in a tongue pray that he may interpret. For if I pray in a tongue, my spirit prays, but my understanding is unfruitful. What is *the conclusion* then? I will pray with the spirit, and I

Witchcraft in the Church

will also pray with the understanding. I will sing with the spirit, and I will also sing with the understanding. Otherwise, if you bless with the spirit, how will he who occupies the place of the uninformed say "Amen" at your giving of thanks, since he does not understand what you say? For you indeed give thanks well, but the other is not edified.
I thank my God I speak with tongues more than you all; yet in the church I would rather speak five words with my understanding, that I may teach others also, than ten thousand words in a tongue.

1 Corinthians 14:13-19

On the night of 22 November 2011 I just could not sleep. I kept on singing with the spirit. This just happens automatically sometimes. I have discovered that when this happens it releases The Holy Spirit in me, upon me and around me. Even when I woke up the next day (Wednesday 23 November 2011) I was still singing with the spirit.

I also discovered that this usually happens the day when something bad is about to happen. My son-in-law came home from work Wednesday night (23 November 2011) at about 7:15pm and told me that he was nearly killed. A forklift came from behind him and if another person did not shout the forks would have pierce his body. He explained it was about 10cm away from his body when it stopped.

On 26 February 2012, I woke up singing with the spirit. That evening my daughter told me how she was nearly involved in two major accidents. The first was a truck that nearly ran over her car but her car was moved supernaturally to the left and the truck went over another car that went over a red light and she was warned to wait a few seconds before she went over the traffic light. If she did not listen to the warning that car would have hit her on the driver side probably killing her. I can only thank God for letting me intercede through singing with the spirit without me even knowing about what was planned. Remember God knows what is planned for us and He will always intercede through us if we are in line with His will.

On 16 November 2012 I woke up singing with the spirit and at about 11am I had the urge to start praying in tongues. About half an hour later my son phoned me to say he was in an accident. A white BMW was overtaking on a bend and they had a head on collision. The pick-up that my son was driving was a write off, but my son was not hurt, he had back pain and some scratches and brushes from the airbags. God had me interceding for my son by singing with the spirit and afterwards praying in tongues.

On 21 November 2012 I woke up singing with the spirit and it continues until 3pm and when it stopped I again had the urge to go and pray at the pulpit. I did not know for who or what I am praying. About 10 minutes later my son phoned me saying he nearly died. My son works on towers that are placed on mountains and hills for internet access. One of the towers was not stable so he and his team were removing the equipment so that they could fix the tower afterwards. On the way down about 15 meters from the ground the tower started tilting and my son had to cut himself loose from the harness and jump to avoid the tower falling on him which would have killed or seriously injured him. He did hurt his back but not as badly as it would have been had he not jumped.

In both these cases of my son (not even a week apart) God had me intercede with singing with the spirit and praying in

Witchcraft in the Church

tongues because Satan planned these accidents for him to have him killed.

You see Satan thought that if he takes one of my children he can once again put a stop to my walk for Christ. He did not succeed this time. Praise God.

On 17 January 1997, Satan had my youngest child killed in a freak accident. It was during a time where I was out of line with God's will and plan for my life.

On 17 January 2013 I was in the area where she was buried and I had to thank God for keeping her safe with Him.

When something bad is about to happen, God intercedes and The Holy Spirit guides me with singing with the spirit. This is awesome. I just know that this is super cool, as my 7 year old grandson would say. I know God loves me a lot and I was told this on so many occasions and I love Him with all my heart and I belong to Him 100% body, soul and spirit forever, nothing will ever change that.

Isn't our God just Awesome. All the Glory to God. Thank you Jesus for dying for our sins on the cross. Thank you Lord Jesus for interceding and surrounding my children every day.

You will see that when I was singing with the spirit, I was singing in my mind but in a language understandable to me.

Hélèné Fulton

Fire of the Holy Spirit

I indeed baptize you with water unto repentance, but He who is coming after me is mightier than I, whose sandals I am not worthy to carry. He will baptize you with the Holy Spirit and fire.

Matthew 3:11

I remember when I first received the Fire on my hands I thought it was an allergic reaction and I rinsed my hands under cold water.

Pastors do not teach the people about the Fire in the churches today. I do not know why as this is so powerful.

On 30 January 2012 I was sleeping next to Jacob but on my side of the bed and there was about a half a meter open space between us.

I was sleeping on my tummy and the next moment I felt a very warm feeling coming over the entire back of my body. I immediately knew that it was the Fire of the Holy Spirit.

Jacob jumped up and said: "You are burning me out" I replied saying that I am not doing anything and that I am not even touching him.

I know that when I am praying for someone my hands starts heating up and the people I have prayed for have told me that even though I do not touch their bodies they could feel the heat in the area that I was praying for and also the heat coming from my hands.

Witchcraft in the Church

I also experience the Fire of the Holy Spirit all over my body when danger or a witch or warlock or Satanist is close to me. I know this is God protecting me.

This is the Fire of the Holy Spirit at work.

Chapter 7: Do not marry him!

The day before I met Jacob, I had a vision. I was standing at a room that belonged to a man and it had [10]dollosses and all sort of African witchcraft accessories in the room.

I did not know about visions back then and though I had an overactive imagination. God was warning me of what was to come and I only realized this 16 years later when I returned to the area where I met him.

God showed me the very same vision again and He said. "My child I warned you 16 years ago that he was not the man that you should marry, but because of a lack of knowledge you did not know. Therefore I want you to teach my children about visions and dreams and how cunning Satan is."

[6] **My people are destroyed for lack of knowledge.**
Because you have rejected knowledge,
I also will reject you from being priest for Me;
Because you have forgotten the law of your God,
I also will forget your children.

Hosea 4:6

My children think that if they do not speak about the devil, he will not attack. My children think that if they do not do witchcraft rituals that they are not involved in witchcraft. Teach my children that they can open themselves up by marrying an unequally yoked person.

Do not be unequally yoked together with unbelievers. For what fellowship has righteousness with lawlessness? And what communion

---

[10] Dollosso is bones and rabit feet and other "things" that witchdoctors use to read a person's feature.

has light with darkness? ¹⁵ And what accord has Christ with Belial? Or what part has a believer with an unbeliever? ¹⁶ And what agreement has the temple of God with idols? For you are the temple of the living God. As God has said:
"I will dwell in them
And walk among them.
I will be their God,
And they shall be My people."
¹⁷ Therefore
"Come out from among them
And be separate, says the Lord.
Do not touch what is unclean,
And I will receive you."
¹⁸ "I will be a Father to you,
And you shall be My sons and daughters,
Says the LORD Almighty."

                                                2 Corinthians 6:14-18

Many people read this passage and assumed that it puts a lot of restrictions on Christian marriages.

This verse does not refer to "marriage" at all. Nonetheless, in principle it certainly applies to marriage.

"Unequally yoked together" is translation from just one Greek word, ***heterozugeo,*** which means, "to yoke up differently; to associate discordantly; unequally yoke together."

The word yoke" is when two oxen are paired together by a pulling beam to do work such as ploughing a field or pulling a wagon

Hélèné Fulton

Paul is telling the Corinthians who was into paganism and who's cities had a lot of pagan temples, that they should not be unequally" yoked with people that practice paganism or any work of darkness.

They were told to avoid: **"unbelievers, unrighteousness, darkness, Belial, infidels, and idols."** This is the exact list Paul gave them, as we read above. Nothing is mentioned about marriage, but it does apply to marriage.

What did Paul mean? It is not possible to live in a country, state, county, city, province or village without constantly coming in contact with people that is into paganism, Satanism or witchcraft. Even Jesus Himself prayed and specified to His Father exactly how He desired for us to live under these circumstances in our life:

I do not pray that You should take them out of the world, but that You should keep them from the evil one.

John 17:15

Jesus was asking that His disciples would not **"be unequally yoked together with unbelievers."**

You can see how important it was to Jesus that we should not be unequally yoked with unbelievers.

It is very important that you fellowship with other believers because then you grow and learn. I have a saying that "the bad corrupt the good". It is so easy for people to rather do the bad things than the good things as satan will make it irresistible for you.

Witchcraft in the Church

Although I have never myself been into witchcraft, because of my marriage with Jacob, satan took that as legal right to attack me and my finances and my family.

There was a time that whenever I was invited to a church and Jacob would accompanying me and they had an alter call, he would go forward. Now to me an alter call is a call for people to give their hearts to the Lord, and you can only become Born Again once.

I asked God to reveal to me why Jacob would go every time and God taught me that sometimes people would say the salvation prayer from their minds but not truly from their hearts.

Jacob had no faith. I remember one specific time I prayed and asked God for R18000 as I needed this to pay the rates and taxes as the money I gave for this was used for something else. The minute I stood up from my knees my phone would ring and a booking at the Bed and breakfast for R18000 was made. I was so excited that my prayer was answered immediately but I was not prepared for what happened next. I was taught a big lesson by God on this day.

I told Jacob that I just prayed for R18000 to pay the rates and taxes bill, I though he will share in my joy and excitement. He went from there to his parents to drink coffee and within 15 minutes the booking was cancelled.

I was devastated and went back on my knees and asked God what happened what I did wrong.

God showed me that during the time that Jacob was at his parents because of all of their (his family) un-believing and negative behaviour they stopped the booking with what they spoke.

There was also one incident I prayed for a man in church for healing and just after I've prayed Jacob said to me you cannot pray for that healing because that is impossible. I was shocked. He immediately cancels my prayer with his words. I had to ask him to leave the room and had to re-pray for the man to get healed.

Let me tell you about my friend. Her son Adam wanted a Corsa [11]Bakkie. So both the parents told him to start praying and asking God for a Corsa Bakkie. Also was praying for about six months when one morning a stranger stopped at their place asking for Adam. The stranger said that I have this almost new Land Cruiser that I never use and God said I must give this to you. Wow. It was not the Corsa Bakkie that Adam prayed for – for six months it was a much better vehicle – much more expensive. Now I must tell you that Adam and our daughter were in Grade 6 together so they are the same age and Adam now is busy with his PHD in Theology because he loves God and wants to do God's work. And believe me Adam was probably one of the naughtiest boys I've ever known. In fact he sat in the corner facing the wall for almost two years in Primary school.

Now let me explain something else to you. Both Adam's parents and his sister Michelle are born again Christians and loves God with all their heart. If while Adam prayed for the Bakkie any of them would have said hahahah you're praying for something that you know you're not going to get or who

---

[11] A smaller type of pick up van

will give you a bakkie or stop praying for things you do not need they would have cancelled Adam's prayers.

[26] If anyone among you[a] thinks he is religious, and does not bridle his tongue but deceives his own heart, this one's religion *is* useless.

James 1:26

Bridle means control.

The tongue can say a lot of things.

If you keep saying this f@#$#@ or that f*&%$ everything that comes out of your mouth and that which is around you will be f&^%$# because the demons will make sure of it. You yourself are cursing the things around you with what you are saying.

In plain English: What you say will happen. So if you say I'm poor. Yes you will be poor. I don't have money. Yes you will not have money; It's going bad with us this month. Yes it will go bad with you this month. These children are so naughty. Yes the children will be naughty. That child is useless. Yes that child will turn out a bum. Saying to a child you're such a [12]sissie, will definitely turn the child into a homosexual. **What you say will happen!!!.**

Death and Life Are in the Power of the Tongue

The verses below will show you just how powerful our words really are and how your words can either be used to bring life, love, edification, and encouragement into a

---

[12] Afrikaans word for saying a boy is like a girl

person's life or bring death, destruction, negativity, and torment.

Death and life *are* in the power of the tongue,
And those who love it will eat its fruit.

Proverbs 18:21

There is one who speaks like the piercings of a sword,
But the tongue of the wise *promotes* health.

Proverbs 12:18

Keep your tongue from evil,
And your lips from speaking deceit.

Psalm 34:13

A man's stomach shall be satisfied from the fruit of his mouth;
From the produce of his lips he shall be filled.

Proverbs 18:20

"The Lord G<small>OD</small> has given Me
The tongue of the learned,
That I should know how to speak
A word in season to *him who is* weary.
He awakens Me morning by morning,
He awakens My ear
To hear as the learned.

Isaiah 50:4

Walk in wisdom toward those *who are* outside, redeeming the time. ⁶ *Let* your speech always *be* with grace, seasoned with salt, that you may know how you ought to answer each one.

Colossians 4:5

The mouth of the righteous *is* a well of life,
But violence covers the mouth of the wicked.

Witchcraft in the Church

Proverbs 10:11

The words of a man's mouth *are* deep waters;
The wellspring of wisdom *is* a flowing brook.

Proverbs 18:4

A wholesome tongue *is* a tree of life,
But perverseness in it breaks the spirit.

Proverbs 15:4

Pleasant words *are like* a honeycomb,
Sweetness to the soul and health to the bones.

Proverbs 16:24

Anxiety in the heart of man causes depression,
But a good word makes it glad.

Proverbs 12:25

A soft answer turns away wrath,
But a harsh word stirs up anger.

Proverbs 15:1

He who guards his mouth preserves his life,
But he who opens wide his lips shall have destruction.

Proverbs 13:3

Whoever guards his mouth and tongue
Keeps his soul from troubles.

Proverbs 21:23

The heart of the righteous studies how to answer,
But the mouth of the wicked pours forth evil.

Proverbs 15:28

Hélèné Fulton

Set a guard, O LORD, over my mouth;
Keep watch over the door of my lips.

Psalm 141:3

Some of these verses have positive benefits and blessings one can receive as the result of learning how to speak properly to others but they also have a warning of negative things that can occur as a result of not properly expressing yourself.

If more people would learn how to walk and abide in the revelation and knowledge and learn how to express themselves in a more positive and godly manner to others, we would have less tensions and conflicts in our marriages, in our families, in our personal friendships, and in the workplace.

Jesus has already told us that those who will live by the sword will also die by the sword. Violence can chase after and literally come upon someone if their speech to others is wicked and evil.

Now we all have families that do not believe. Many of our relatives would say I am a Christian but they never read their Bible. The closes they come to reading their Bibles is seeing a Bible verse posted on Facebook or send out as a Blackberry message. They might only see the inside of a church at a wedding or a funeral. But if you ask them they are a Christian. I like to call these types of people "casual Christians". They have no faith and no personal relationship with God. They only believe there is a God. They do not know the true meaning or understand what Jesus has done for them. They do not even know about the Holy Spirit. And many of them think that if they do not bother the devil he will not bother them.

Witchcraft in the Church

Well they are right on one thing there. If they do not read their Bible and pray and get to know Jesus personally then Satan has no reason to bother them as they are working for him and they are doing his works. Believe me the minute that they start reading their Bibles and start praying Satan will be jumping up because he will be losing a soul and that is the minute he will start fighting you. While you in the world and doing the things of the world he (Satan) has no reason to worry about you. But being in this world will mean that you will go to hell when you die. So the choice is yours. Eternal life with God in heaven or eternal damnation with Satan in hell.

Let's look at another very important point that God pointed out to me in this marriage with Jacob.

God showed me that when you marry someone you became one in flesh but also in spiritual world and if the one is an unbeliever Satan will have the legal right to attack the other believing spouse. Also remember that when you marry someone you immediately also inherit their entire bloodline and are link to that bloodline. Think about it. If that bloodline has a curse on it, that curse is now on you unless it is broken.

From day one in my marriage with Jacob, I was not welcomed by his family. My children were not welcome. Jacob's mother always made a point of it to point out that my children are the stepchildren. Now in God's eyes when you marry it became your children and family.

Becoming one was so important to God that a verse on it appears 4 times in the Bible.

Hélèné Fulton

Therefore a man shall leave his father and mother and be joined to his wife, and they shall become one flesh.

Genesis 2:24

and said, 'For this reason a man shall leave his father and mother and be joined to his wife, and the two shall become one flesh'?

Matthew 19:5

For this reason a man shall leave his father and mother and be joined to his wife,

Mark 10:7

"For this reason a man shall leave his father and mother and be joined to his wife, and the two shall become one flesh."

Ephesians 5:31

Unfortunately Jacob was never prepared to truly convert and accept Jesus as his Lord and Savior.

God revealed to me that Jacob's daughter had a Jezebel spirit.

On 9 February 2011 the day after he walked out on me saying he want nothing to do with me or God she came into my office to beg me to take him back. I told her that I did not walk out on him, he walked out on me. She said she is sorry and will try harder to like me.

I asked her why is it that she did the things she did. She asked what things. I asked her well for starters why do you always cause a fight. Why do you always bring out other peoples wrong doings to save yourself. Why don't you just admit what you have done and say you are sorry. Why do you tell so much lies. Why did you say someone molested you just because he made a joke that he is going to hit your father because he does not come to visit? Why do you drink so much? Why do you want to seduce married men? Why do you dress so revealing? You even came with a see through white top and a short which looked like a hot pants to church and the congregation wanted to know why I allow this.

The only answer I got from her was that she enjoys it when a man gets an erection looking at her as it gives her power over them.

I was shocked!

On 8 February 2012 God gave me 1 Corinthians 7:15 after Jacob walked out on our marriage for the 7th time. He left with the words: "He wants nothing to do with God or with me."

> But if the unbeliever departs, let him depart; a brother or a sister is not under bondage in such *cases*. But God has called us to peace.
> **1 Corinthians 7:15**

This gave me permission from God to end the marriage. I filed for divorce but God had one more surprise in store for me.

Even though I filed for the divorce and was supposed to divorce him. In the end God turned the proceedings supernaturally around and Jacob was the one who divorced me by having to stand up in court saying he wants to end the marriage.

I spoke to Jacob about 7 weeks after he left me and told him that I forgive him and that Jesus loves him. He told me to stuff Jesus's love up my behind in much more colourful words than what I am using.

On another occasion I told him that God will forgive him if he repent and accept Jesus as his Lord and Savior.

I told him that there is help for his daughter as well.

He told me that he loves his daughter more than God.

37 He who loves father or mother more than Me is not worthy of Me. And he who loves son or daughter more than Me is not worthy of Me.
Matthew 10:37

Witchcraft in the Church

Chapter 8: Followed from Hell (Hades)

6 April 2011

I was asked by Jane, a spiritual daughter to help a young man, Pieter aged 20. Pieter manifested with goat claws and red eyes in the church and the church pastor asked Jane to ask me to do deliverance on Pieter.

We spend an entire week to prepare for the deliverance. During this week I fasted from midnight to noon with water only. I asked God to give me the prayers to pray for Pieter and to show and teach me what I needed to know in order to set Pieter free from bondage. My spiritual daughter, Jane was also doing the same during this time.

We drove to Empangeni to do the deliverance on Pieter.

Before we entered the house I bind the demons so that we could have a peaceful deliverance.

I was saying this out loud. I bind every demon that reign inside this house and inside the people that is inside the house in the name of Jesus Christ.

Father God please wash me and Jane with the blood of Jesus and clothe us with Your full armour as per Ephesians 6. Father God, baptise Jane and I with the Fire of the Holy Spirit. I pray this in the name of Jesus Christ. Amen

Hélèné Fulton

After I've said this prayer we entered Susan, Pieter's sister's house. Pieter's mother Magdalene was present. Magdalene was Caucasian, but Pieter looked more Indian. His skin was very dark in colour and I thought that maybe his father is mixed race.

I asked Pieter, when he first noticed this "thing" and this was Pieter's reply: "I first noticed this thing when I overdosed 4 years back on drugs. This thing followed me back from "hell".

I remember I wanted to cry but could not do this in front of Pieter and his mother. I could see that my spiritual daughter, Jane, was also very close to crying when she heard this.

Note that Pieter could answer my questions because the demon was in chains and fetters and they could not interfere or stop him.

God gave me the following prayers and Pieter had to say them out loud with his eyes open. The reason for the open eyes was so that Satan could not say that Pieter was asleep and not aware of what he was doing.

God showed me that there where generational curses on the mother. So I asked both Pieter and his mother, Magdalene to say the following prayer out loud with their eyes open.

In the name of Jesus Christ I confess all the sins of my forefathers, and by the redemptive blood of Jesus, I now break the power of every curse passed down to me through my ancestral line. I confess and repent of each and every sin that I have committed, known or unknown, and accept Christ's forgiveness. He has redeemed me from the curse of the law. I choose the blessing and reject the curse. In the name of my

Lord Jesus Christ, I break the power of every evil curse spoken against me. I cancel the force of every prediction spoken about me, whether intentionally or carelessly, that was not according to God's promised blessings. I bless those who have cursed me. I forgive each person who has ever wronged me or spoken evil of me. In the name of Jesus Christ, I command every evil spirit of curse to leave me now.

In the name of the Lord Jesus Christ, I now renounce, break and loose myself from all demonic subjection to my mother, my father, my grandparents and any other human beings, living or dead, who have dominated and controlled me in any way. I thank You, Lord, for setting me free.

Then I asked Pieter to say the following prayer after me also out loud with his eyes open.

In the name of Jesus Christ I now rebuke, break and loose myself, from any and all evil operating through my drug abuse and through the games I played. I command all such demonic powers to leave me in the name of Jesus Christ. I am the head and not the tail. I am above and not beneath.

In the name of the Lord Jesus Christ, I now renounce, break and loose myself from all demonic soul ties formed through sinful sexual encounters. I accept God's forgiveness. In the name of Jesus Christ, I command all demons associated with perverse soul ties to go.

Lord Jesus Christ, I believe that you are the Son of God. You are the Saviour that came in the flesh to destroy the works of the devil. You died on the cross for my sins and rose up from the dead. I now confess all of my sins, known and unknown, and repent of each one. I ask You Lord Jesus Christ to forgive me and cleanse me in Your blood. I do believe that Your blood cleanses me now from all sin. Thank You for redeeming me, cleansing me, and sanctifying me in Your blood. I pray this in Jesus Christ name. I come to you, Jesus Christ, as my Deliverer. You know all my problems - the things that bind me, that torment me, that defile and harass me. I now loose myself from every dark spirit, from every evil influence, from every satanic bondage, from every spirit in me that is not the Spirit of God, and I command all such spirits to leave me now, in the name Jesus Christ. I now invite the Holy Spirit to fill me and guide me. I now confess that my body is a temple of the Holy Spirit, redeemed, cleansed and sanctified by the blood of Jesus. Therefore, Satan has no place in me, and no power over me, through the blood of Jesus. I pray this in the name of Jesus Christ. Amen

After this last prayer I asked Pieter how he feels. Pieter said that he felt so free and clean. He said he feels so warm and that he previously always felt cold. Pieter also said that he was so afraid of not doing what this demon told him because if he did not listen the demon will hurt him or his family.

I told Pieter that it is very important that he will equip himself with the Word of God (the Bible) otherwise this demon will come back and bring 7 stronger than the demon we cast out and he will be worse off than now.

Witchcraft in the Church

An Unclean Spirit Returns

"When an unclean spirit goes out of a man, he goes through dry places, seeking rest, and finds none. Then he says, 'I will return to my house from which I came.' And when he comes, he finds *it* empty, swept, and put in order. Then he goes and takes with him seven other spirits more wicked than himself, and they enter and dwell there; and the last *state* of that man is worse than the first. So shall it also be with this wicked generation."

Matthew 12:43-45

Others, testing *Him,* sought from Him a sign from heaven. But He, knowing their thoughts, said to them: "Every kingdom divided against itself is brought to desolation, and a house *divided* against a house falls. If Satan also is divided against himself, how will his kingdom stand? Because you say I cast out demons by Beelzebub. And if I cast out demons by Beelzebub, by whom do your sons cast *them* out? Therefore they will be your judges. But if I cast out demons with the finger of God, surely the kingdom of God has come upon you. When a strong man, fully armed, guards his own palace, his goods are in peace. But when a stronger than he comes upon him and overcomes him, he takes from him all his armor in which he trusted, and divides his spoils. He who is not with Me is against Me, and he who does not gather with Me scatters.

An Unclean Spirit Returns

"When an unclean spirit goes out of a man, he goes through dry places, seeking rest; and finding none, he says, 'I will return to my house from which I came.' And when he comes, he finds *it* swept and put in order. Then he goes and takes with *him* seven other spirits more wicked than himself, and they enter and dwell there; and the last *state* of that man is worse than the first."

Luke 11:16-26

Hélèné Fulton

10 months after the deliverance I was prompted by the Holy Spirit to contact Pieter and his mother. I immediately left messages everywhere. Two days later Magdalene, Pieter's mother contacted me via email and said that she and Pieter need to come and see me. I was on tour spreading the word of God so I told her that I will let her know when I am in Durban area.

2 months later Pieter's sister signed up for the Prayer Academy and invited me on BBM (Blackberry), I did not know it was his sister.

On 10 May 2013, I received an Invite from Pieter's mother after Susan, Pieter's sister told me that I did a deliverance on her brother in Empangeni. I immediately knew it was Pieter as this was a huge victory for the Kingdom of God.

Pieter's mother told me that she was helping an atheist to type his book and that during this time she started to believe that there is no God. She even packed away her Bible and stopped going to church.

Now this is what always shocks me as people that has seen the power of God at work, like Magdalene saw on the day of her deliverance and her son Pieter's deliverance, can be deceived by Satan in believing that there is no God.

I asked God how this is possible and God gave me the verse below. God said that Satan is so full of pride that he thinks he is god.

Satan Tempts Jesus
Then Jesus was led up by the Spirit into the wilderness to be tempted by the devil.

Matthew 4:1

Witchcraft in the Church

People want to see a physical god and not a Supernatural God. And Satan uses this to his advantage. It is not Magdalene's fault. Therefore we should be very careful what we read and to whom we open our ears to.

Satan even tried to tempt Jesus. We need to be so careful not to be deceived by the devil. Therefore Gods Word tells us to resist the devil.

Therefore submit to God. Resist the devil and he will flee from you.
James 4:7

On 10 May 2013 Magdalene spent the weekend with her daughter Susan and son Pieter and Susan showed her a video of Mary K Baxter. Magdalene realized that she was wrong and repented and asked God to forgive her for doubting that God exists.

On 11 May 2013 Magdalene told me that she had a dream and in the dream a big black dragon is covering the house where Pieter and his sister lived.

She said that she immediately had the urge to cover them with the blood of Jesus. This was the correct thing to do. I also told her to cancel the dream by saying the following out loud.

I rebuke and cancel the dream I had where I saw a big black dragon with red eyes covering the house of my children in the name of Jesus Christ.

Hélèné Fulton

13 months after the deliverance, I asked Pieter to explain to me how he saw the demon, while the demon was inside of him.

Pieter said that it was a bit difficult to explain what it looked like as the demon pretended to be something he is not. Pieter said that the demon looked like a mountain goat standing on two legs, but without the hair on the face. He had red eyes and goat claws. He had a flat nose and he had goat horns.

Pieter said that when the demon got angry, he looked like a big black dragon with big wings and red eyes.

Pieter said that this demon spoke Latin to him. I asked Pieter if he understood what the demon said to him when the demon spoke Latin to him. Pieter said that it was very weird as although he can only speak broken English and Afrikaans, he could understand every word this demon spoke to him in Latin.

So the great dragon was cast out, that serpent of old, called the Devil and Satan, who deceives the whole world; he was cast to the earth, and his angels were cast out with him.

Revelation 12:9

Pieter also told me that sometimes the demon was inside of him and then he was doing things and he could never remember what he did and the family had to tell him. He said that when the demon was not inside of him he was always next to him. He could always see him.

I asked Susan, Pieter's sister to tell me some of the things Pieter did when the demon was inside of him.

Witchcraft in the Church

Susan said that Pieter one day ran his head into the wall and that some of the men put him on a chair and tried to hold him still. She said that Pieter's eyes turned black and he started laughing in a strange voice. He told them in this strange voice in English (note their native tongue is Afrikaans) that they are all going to hell. They gave him some sugar water to calm him but he spat it out. They tried to bring the Bible closer to him but he just kept on laughing. This went on for 2 hours.

Susan said that when the demon was inside Pieter he spoke English as if it is his native tongue. She also told me that Pieter's English is so bad on a normal day and that this was one of the many things that stood out for her.

He also manifested inside a church with red eyes and goat claws as hands.

Satan is trying to get back in and I told the family that they need to read their Bible and pray and keep themselves filled with the Holy Spirit and stay in line with God.

Hélèné Fulton

Chapter 9: Her health for his wealth

On Friday 30 January 2012, I had to find out that the father involved another pastor to do the deliverance which I was preparing for, with the help of the Holy Spirit for nearly 2 months and the deliverance would have taken place only later that week after prayer and fasting and with the go ahead from the Holy Spirit, but when I tried to explain this to Jacob and Wazeem the father of the child, I heard the Holy Spirit say that they will not listen and that I must just let it go.

Just as we are about to leave the house on that Sunday morning, I clearly heard the Holy Spirit tell me to take an extra pair of shoes. I remember thinking but these shoes are new they will not break, but I did take an extra pair of shoes - a pair of flats as the shoes I had on had heels.

As we climbed out of the car I stepped into dog poo. I had no choice then but to put the other pair of shoes on. It was a good thing as the service and deliverance went on for hours and I would not have been able to concentrate with aching feet. At this stage I still had a lot of pain in my feet from a curse that was placed on me from Jacob and his family.

When I arrived at this church the music was overwhelmingly loud that you could not hear what were they singing and it really freaked out the family a bit. Alisha did not want to enter the church and I had to bind the demons so that she could enter the church. From this moment Alisha just wanted to be with me and hold my hand. I knew she saw Jesus Christ in me and because of this she felt safe.

Witchcraft in the Church

I noticed that inside the church were Christmas decorations and a Christmas tree. I just knew when I saw these decorations that this church has no discernment or clue about true deliverance as this is a pagan tradition and not a Christian tradition. The pagan's celebrated Christmas with trees and decorations. More about this in my book Beware Pagan Traditions & False Religions.

Then half the congregation started doing the deliverance by shouting and screaming and asking the demons what are your names etc. I do not want to go into much detail, but it is not how I was taught by the Holy Spirit to do deliverance. During this time Alisha was very scared and was reaching out to me the entire time. I was just standing and watching as God did not tell me to go ahead. The pastor told me to go and stand outside as I am distracting the child.

I asked God what was going on and if it were true that I was distracting the child. God said to me: "No my child she sees Jesus in you and that makes her want to be with you as she feels safe with you. These people are not really doing deliverance; they just want to put up a show. Take the mother first and lead her back to Me as she was once My child but has accepted false gods when she married the husband."

I took the mother outside and she confirmed what God said that she was once a devoted child of God but took the husbands religion when she married him. The mother said the following prayer.

"Father God, I acknowledge that I have stepped out of line from Your will for me. I have sinned, I have turned to

false gods, even though you clearly tell me in Your Word not to worship false gods, but Father I know that Jesus Christ died for my sins on the cross and that if I am truly sorry and repent that You will forgive me. Father God please forgive me my sins, those that are known and unknown to me and wash me as white as snow with the blood of Jesus Christ. Holy Spirit I invite You to come and live inside of Me and guide and comfort me. I ask this in the name of Jesus Christ. Amen."

I asked God if I am distracting the child and deliverance and God said no my dear child you are the only person here that has the authority to do that deliverance and the child is seeing the love of Jesus in you that is why she wants to be with you as she feels safe. My heart was torn to pieces as I felt so sorry for that child and just wanted to help her, but God said that I should be calm and just do as He says otherwise it will harm the child more than help her.

I could hear Jacob constantly asking the demons what are their names and I just know that God does not want us to speak to the demons unless He commands us to do so.

At 11am when the deliverance started Alisha had 9 major demons inside of her and as you know most of these major demons each have their own legions of smaller demons that can be up to 1000 sometimes even more.

By 3:30 pm 2 demons and their legions where cast out. These were small demons and they were only willing to go to satisfy the pastor and make the congregation believe that they succeeded with the deliverance.

We went home as I was not needed according to that pastor.

Witchcraft in the Church

When I got back home I took an afternoon nap at about 5pm and I was attacked by a demon. I was lying on my tummy and this demon attacked me from the back. I could not speak. So everything I said here was in my mind (spirit).

I could not move. I said get off from me I am covered with the blood of Jesus Christ, but the demon did not move. I then said that I have the full armor of God on as per Ephesians 6. Again the demon did not move. I then remember that two nights prior I received the Fire of the Holy Spirit on my back. I say I am baptized with the Fire of the Holy Spirit and immediately the demon left.

That night I had a vision about the father of the family just after my prayer.

In the vision was Jesus Christ's hands and I could see His prayer shawl. He was busy molding the family (sort of like the potter and clay) on top of this I saw the pyramid with the 3rd eye and on top of this (like the Illuminati) I saw a sun with a face. Meaning: Jesus Christ wants to work with this family but the father has not accepted Him completely.

I visit the family and Alisha during the week following, she still needs a lot of deliverance. Because the deliverance could not be completed the father is now a little skeptic as he only accepted Jesus Christ as His Savior yesterday, but due to all of this wants to keep his options open, so he does not want to get rid of all his false gods. Believe me they are everywhere, and not just Hindu, he even had Buddha etc. Alisha is also struck with the demon of muteness and is not talking since May 2011.

Last night the father was physically struck with muteness and was attacked and could not call out to his wife and phoned her at 1:30 pm. This morning the father is still in shock as you would understand. Can you see why God showed me the vision?

The Holy Spirit reminded me that I need to pray and fast for 3 days. So I will be doing the deliverance only after the 3rd day of fasting with only water. I have asked another Prayer Eagle to assist me in this deliverance and she will also be fasting with me. I will send out her name with an intercessor prayer for us. For now I'd like you to continue to stand in the Gap for Alisha and I want you also to start praying for the father Wazeem Naidoo that he will come to see that Jesus Christ is the only way.

The first thing you need to understand when praying for the lost is that the price has been paid. When Jesus Christ died upon that cross He paid the price for every single sinner on the earth. When you are praying for the lost remember that the price has been paid and make that the starting point for prayer.

"Lord you bought Wazeem Naidoo at Calvary, he is yours and so is his wife Silvia Naidoo and now we are asking You to claim Wazeem and Silvia for yourself, to remove the chains that bind them. Don't let the Devil have those you have bought Lord, be glorified in them and through them Lord. Take them back to yourself, set them free; Christ has

Knowing that Christ has paid the price gives us confidence to pray boldly. It is not as if we have to bargain at all. The price is paid - that person rightly belongs to God who has bought them back out of slavery and sin. The technical name for this is "praying on the basis of redemption" or in some circles "praying for the lost in the power of the blood of Jesus" . Stand before God, confident that He wants your friend saved and confident that He has already paid the price for that to happen.

PERSISTENTLY AND REGULARLY - praying for people to be saved can at times be a very long battle. We need to pray persistently and regularly for those we want to be saved. In Luke 18:1

Jesus makes it clear that persistence pays off and tells us that we ought to "pray and not get weary.."

PRAY WATCHFULLY - It pays to be alert to the spiritual state of the unbeliever and to pray appropriately - are they curious about God yet? Are they convicted about their sin? Are they attracted to Jesus? Are they involved in something they would find very difficult to give up if they became a Christian? Pray specifically for where the person is at spiritually so they can take one or two steps closer to faith in God. "Lord you know how Wazeem finds it hard to believe your Bible - please show him it is true and that it can be relied on..." Lord Jesus please visit Wazeem and show him your hands and feet and Your love for him.

Chapter 10: Attacks

In this chapter I am going to give you an account of various times where I and others came under attack through the work of the enemy. You will see how important faith and spiritual warfare is in combating the enemy by using the blood of Jesus Christ and the Sword of the Spirit - the Word of God.

These are some of the more serious attacks:
I dreamt that my house and car were sliding into the river and the next moment I was standing on the veranda of the main house and I was looking down to where my house was standing and all I could see is the roof of my house and my car floating next to my house. The road between my house and the main house was full of deep craters because of all the water.

I cancelled and renounced the dream and all the evil that was planned through this dream in the name of Jesus Christ.

Attack in October 2011

Our church services were at 2pm every Sunday. The family returned from church to pack the picnic baskets as we had a potjie (a potjie is a traditional South African meal made in a black 3 legged pot over coals. It has meat and different layers of vegetable, sort of like a casserole) planned at the beach after church with the rest of the congregation.

I was called to the main house as a small yellow bird had appeared out of nowhere and was inside the birdcage with the two cockatiels. No one was home to put this bird into the cage.

Witchcraft in the Church

I recall the kids making fun and jokes saying that the two cockatiels were lonely and they said "come on in tweety."

Although I found it very strange, I did not think anything bad about it as it was a small little yellow bird. Almost like a canary. Very pretty. All my children and I are animal lovers and we always have animals around.

We went to the beach with the rest of the congregation.

All through this week, Simon, Tammy and I kept on talking about how strange it is that this bird just appeared out of nowhere. If it were a bird that got lost from someone else's house, as we stayed next to a nature reserve and we do get this a lot, the bird would have been outside the cage and we would have had to catch it, but the fact that the bird was inside the cage was the strange part.

On the Friday night I saw how the main house was picked up by a small yellow bird in the spiritual world. I rebuked it in the name of Jesus Christ. I heard from Tammy about two months later as we discussed the "yellow bird" that Simon her husband, had a similar vision of the yellow bird carrying the main house away around the same time I did.

The Saturday morning when we woke up, the yellow bird was gone from the birdcage the bird totally disappeared as mysteriously as it appeared.

Saturday evening, the kids decided to have a potjie again and invited some of our friends over, just three families. One of the families was Pastor Koos from the Full Gospel church. We did not discuss the yellow bird with anyone outside our direct family, but Pastor Koos said to me "Hélèné, how would you like a pretty yellow bird" I just said to him that I do not like yellow. I found it very strange that he would even mention "yellow bird", unless he is connected to the dark side in the spiritual world.

I had this uneasy feeling about him ever since Hester the witch told him about me and he first came and visited me in my office. I felt that there is something strange and dark about him.

He would come to our church services and then take the congregation members mobile numbers and addresses and then visit them at home without making an appointment.

We had a young couple that just started their walk with the Lord. They had two young children a boy and a girl. The girl used to have an "imaginary friend" this friend disappeared since they were getting spiritual food from us and one of my spiritual brothers and his wife.

After the visit from this pastor and one of his elders (this man said to my face he does not believe in the Supernatural healing), the "imaginary friend" re-appeared to the little girl. Unfortunately the couple got such a fright by other things they also seen after the visit that we lost them and they stop coming to church.

This pastor and his elder also visited another couple who that night had to rebuke the spirit of Epilepsy in their 2 year old son. The son never had these attacks before and also never after this one time incident. The Holy Spirit took over and the father rebuked this evil spirit of Epilepsy in tongues. This father never spoke in tongues before.

One of the attacks involving a Black Cat

Just 3 days after the yellow bird tried to carry the main house away. I was walking down to the bottom house (It is only 40 meters apart), I noticed a black cat rubbing itself on the corner of the bottom house. This is the house that I stayed in and where my office was situated. I immediately was told by the God that I should claim back the bottom house by anointing all four corners of the house and saying the following words out loud.

In the name of the Father, the Son and the Holy Ghost, I claim back this house as it was given to me by God my Father whom I serve and love. I rebuke this black cat that came walking and rubbing itself on the corner of my house as if the house belongs to it, in the name of Jesus Christ. Amen.

Tormented for 22 years

19 November 2011

On Monday night while sleeping I suddenly was woken up by God as there was an evil presence in my room. As I opened my eyes this huge greenish demon was standing looking at me. I took my pillow hitting it and while hitting it, rebuking it and telling it to leave me alone in the name of Jesus Christ. It left immediately when I mentioned Jesus' name.

Hélèné Fulton

I know what you all are thinking – crazy lady – well the family and spiritual children are still laughing. Being tormented and bothered for an entire week by demons was no fun but God has allowed this so that I will know what others are going through.

26 November 2011, I had a call from a man who was being tormented by demons for more than 22 years. I've already been shown he has an anointing on him and this is why God made me go through this so that I can feel this man and others pain and frustration. Remember demons cannot enter me because the Holy Spirit lives inside of me and I am born again and in line with God's will. But they did enter this poor man. I did the deliverance on him on the 27th.

This man was attack by demons that looked like a cross between a fruit fly and a mosquito and they made the skin itchy. He was also attack by snake like demons. He had a distinct bad odour on his body and also a very bad smell in his mouth. The man said he noticed this odour the minute he started to watch pornographic movies and start sleeping with protitutes.

By the grace of God this man was delivered completely and is now an Evangelist.

Threads from Satan

On 9 December 2011 I received this email.

{WORLD SPIRITUAL LEADER}.
HI DEAR.

IT WILL BE A SURPRISE TO YOU WHY THIS MASSAGE WAS SEND TO YOU, YES IT WAS REVIEW ON

Witchcraft in the Church

SPIRITUAL WORLD CONSIGNING YOUR LIFE AND DEATH AS YOUR LIFE HAS COMING TO END WITHIN 45 DAYS AHEAD, IT WAS REVIEW IN SPIRITUAL WORLD,

THIS ARE THE REASON WHY YOU WILL DIE IN 45 DAY AHEAD, IF YOU HAVE SPIRITUAL EYES YOU WILL OBSERVE THIS AND DON'T NEGLECT THIS SPIRITUAL REVIEW FROM SPIRITUAL WORLD, KINDLY TELL ANYONE BY YOUR SIDE SO WHEN THE EVENT WILL COME TO FULFILLED IT WILL NOT BE SURPRISE,

A NEW BORN BABE CHILD HAS TAKING YOUR POSITION IN SPIRITUAL WORLD BEEN GRANT TO BE BORN IN OUT SIDE WORLD IN ORDER TO REPLACE YOUR LIFE, BUT YOU HAVE ONLY ONE ALTERNATIVE TO AVOID HIS COMING TO

THE WORLD IN ORDER FOR YOU TO HAVE HIS LIFE ADDING INTO YOUR LIFE, YOU HAVE TO SACRIFICE IN YOUR HOME AND IN THE SPIRITUAL WORLD WITH INSTRUCTION OF THE {SPIRITUAL LEADER}

                                        {YOUR LIFE OR DEATH}
                                    {WORLD SPIRITUAL LEADER}

I replied back with the following words. I rebuke you in the name of Jesus Christ, my Lord and Savior. God has anointed me to save souls and I am not afraid of you. I will not do a sacrifice for you! I will not die as God protects me because I am His servant.

Hélèné Fulton
Satan stealing her babies

2 February 2012

Below is an email I received from one of the Prayer Academy students.

Last night I had a strange dream. I am pregnant, 16 weeks, now I dreamt like I wanted to go into labor though it wasn't my time yet, my sister accompanied me, I was given an injection if not a sedative so that the pregnancy grows big and I could go to labor ward to deliver, then it was like I was waiting to go to theatre. I felt so uneasy in the dream. I woke up made a small prayer canceling the whole dream in the name of Jesus. What is the meaning of this? I was operated before, because I had fibroids in my uterus, and the doctors expectations are that I deliver through c-section again. The experience was just awful and painful. I am confused.

See my reply below
Satan is trying to steal your baby.
Please say out loud: Satan, you're a thief and I rebuke you trying to steal my baby by letting your demons pose as my sister and as medical staff. I cancel this dream and all the evil plans you had with this dream in the mighty name of Jesus Christ.
Lord Jesus please wash my baby with Your Blood and please protect my pregnancy so that I will carry full term and give birth without extreme pain or any complications. I pray this in Jesus' name. Amen

Witchcraft in the Church

The snake

On 31 January 2012, I was kneeling in prayer next to my bed when I saw a vision of a black Mamba right by my mouth trying to listen what I am praying about.

On 8 February 2012, Jacob walked out on me saying he wanted nothing to do with me or with God.

On 9 February 2012, my friend came over for a visit and to borrow a book from me on spiritual warfare.

We were sitting in my office drinking coffee when Jacob walked into the house and sat down on the couch next to the book shelve. I asked him if I can help him with anything. He left via another door about ten minutes later.

My friend and I went to the bookshelf about 45 minutes later and I sat on the exact same spot as Jacob did earlier as it was right next to the bookshelf. I suddenly felt a sharp pain on my ankle and when I looked down I saw a black mamba. I immediately rebuke it in the name of Jesus Christ and neutralise the poison with the Blood of Jesus.

My friend left about half an hour later. Immediately God said to me: "Anoint your house". I obeyed God immediately. Then God said to me close your doors which I did. I forgot that my office window was open.

About an hour later my brother came down to my house and looked through my office window. This is the exact words that followed.

Hélèné Fulton

Do you know that there is a snake making its way into your house? I told him that No I did not but let me open the door and I will kill it. My brother then told me that if I open the door the snake will strike as it is already in a strike position. I said well then I will climb through the window and kill it from the outside.

By the time I got the ladder to climb out of the window my brother and son-in-law already killed the snake.

God said to me burn the snake and take photos. You could clearly see the human projection in the flames.

I had to get an interdict against Jacob because of his threads to me. His daughter went to the same court and got an counter interdict against me saying I am a witch and that she fears for her and her father's life. This after the police had to remove his guns and put it into safe keeping. With her interdict she prevented me from entering my house where I was running a backpacker and BnB.

It is amazing at what is going on in the justice system. On the day that we appeared in front of a judge in her office, the daughter wanted the judge to order me to pay her (22 years old) maintenance. She said that she and her father had no money. The judge asked her what she is doing. She said she works for her father in his business. The judge asked her how is it possible that she works for her father in his business but claims she has no money and wanted me that does not earn a salary and was prevented from operating my business to pay her.

On another question from the judge she answered that there are a lot of dangerous snakes on our premises. The father quickly whispered to her to keep her mouth shut.

Frogs

About 3 weeks after this my children and I went out to the movies. On our return we found an army of frogs. I told my son-in-law to not let any of those frogs into my house. One of the frogs jumped over 7 meters right into my house and immediately hide behind the fridge. I rebuked the frogs in the name of Jesus Christ and they all disappear.

Frogs represents demonic works.

Attacks involving Sofia

During 2009, Katlego asked me to go and pray for her sister, Sofia, as she is very ill. According to x-rays she had sores on her spine and she was too weak to go to the hospital with a taxi.

I asked God to give me the prayers to pray and I visited Sofia at her home. I let her say the prayers out loud and I also explain the salvation prayer and Sofia said the salvation prayer and became born again.

A week later Katlego told me that her sister is healed completely. She went to the hospital and the x-rays showed no sores on her spine. She said the doctors were amazed and could not understand how this is possible. As they basically told her there is nothing they can do for her and she will have to go and die at home.

I praise God as all glory belongs to our Father. I am only a vessel doing His will.

A few months later Katlego got a better offer and her sister Sofia started working for me in her place.

I had a dream of Simon going onto a big hill and he was busy doing something on a table with some instruments on it. Whatever he was doing caused lightning.

Then he came down from the hill and told me that he needs to go to a higher hill to get more power and more lightning. I asked if I can come with as I want to learn and he said no.

Then a group of black teenagers dressed in school uniforms came down from the hill where Simon was and when they were close to me I asked them what did you do and the one answered me and said: "We buried Sofia as she has died." Sofia worked for me as a domestic worker.

This dream bothered me for a while and I asked God to show me what it is about.

Then about a month after this Sofia suddenly started treating me bad as if I am the worker and she is the madam of the house. I did not even had the time to ask her what is wrong as two days later she did not return to work.

I discovered that a lot of my jewellery was gone as well as my digital (worth about R3800) was also missing and an extra cellular phone I had.

Witchcraft in the Church

The one night 5 June 2012, John a visiting pastor had a dream of a young black girl that took my jewellery and other things from my house. We did cancel and renounce the dream. I asked him to describe the young lady and from his description I recognised Sofia.

On 20 June 2012, I received a Whatsapp message from Sofia saying that for the past 4 nights she has been dreaming the same dream of me. I asked her what the dream was about and she told me that I am in a very deep hole in the ground and I am crying and praying but it is too deep for me to climb out.

I told her to cancel and renounce the dream and at the same time I cancel and renounce the dream out loud in the name of Jesus Christ.

I had another visiting pastor with me and when I looked down I had mud under my finger nails. This was very strange as I have not been near mud or working in a garden for days.

I ask God to show me what is going on.

I received several visions. Jacob had sex with Sofia and because he no longer wanted anything to do with her after he had his way, she started treating me bad when she was still working for me and then she took some of my jewellery and other belongings as she felt she deserve something from him. Just like Hagar treated Sarah.

Hélèné Fulton

In October 2012, I received a phone call from Katlego, Sofia's sister saying she was in hospital and all her organs are failing. Sofia was in a semi coma at the time.
I was almost 680km from her and I asked Katlego to phone me when she is at the hospital and to put the phone on speaker close to Sofia.

I was only prompted to say the following words led by the Holy Spirit.

Sofia, ask God for forgiveness for what you have done as I have already forgiven you. Ten minutes later Sofia died. I knew she was born again and needed to make things right with God.

The Worship Team

On 12 June 2012 I had a dream of some of the congregation members going on a bus trip in a yellow bus, an old yellow bus the type used for school. We stopped at a river bank and my 5 year old grandson was playing in the water but from the shore side, he was naked. When I asked his parents where his clothes were they said that the monkey took it. I then saw a monkey in the yellow bus. When I woke up I renounced and cancelled the dream.

Now we have a man and women who are leading our worship. The man had 23 years in deliverance ministry. They are not married but are living together – according to them "married before God" despite the man not even being divorced from his wife. The wife cheated on him and is living with another man. I am not judging but to me this is wrong as the Bible says we should obey God's laws and the Government's laws. To me common-sense says that even though his wife cheated he must be divorced legally before he gets married to someone else. And they live in a yellow bus, exactly like the one in my dream.

Submit to Government
13 Let every soul be subject to the governing authorities. For there is no authority except from God, and the authorities that exist are appointed by God. ² Therefore whoever resists the authority resists the ordinance of God, and those who resist will bring judgment on themselves. ³ For rulers are not a terror to good works, but to evil. Do you want to be unafraid of the authority? Do what is good, and you will have praise from the same. ⁴ For he is God's minister to you for good. But if you do evil, be afraid; for he does not bear the sword in vain; for he is God's minister, an avenger to *execute* wrath on him who practices evil. ⁵ Therefore *you* must be subject, not only because of wrath but also for conscience' sake. ⁶ For because of this you also pay taxes, for they are God's ministers attending continually to this very thing. ⁷ Render therefore to all their due: taxes to whom taxes *are due,* customs to whom customs, fear to whom fear, honor to whom honor.

Love Your Neighbor
⁸ Owe no one anything except to love one another, for he who loves another has fulfilled the law. ⁹ For the commandments, "You shall not commit adultery," "You shall not murder," "You shall not steal," "You shall not bear false witness," "You shall not covet," and if *there is* any other commandment, are *all* summed up in this saying, namely, "You shall love your neighbor as yourself." ¹⁰ Love does no harm to a neighbor; therefore love *is* the fulfillment of the law.

Put on Christ
¹¹ And *do* this, knowing the time, that now *it is* high time to awake out of sleep; for now our salvation *is* nearer than when we *first* believed. ¹² The night is far spent, the day is at hand. Therefore let us cast off the works of darkness, and let us put on the armor of light. ¹³ Let us walk properly, as in the day, not in revelry and

drunkenness, not in lewdness and lust, not in strife and envy. [14] But put on the Lord Jesus Christ, and make no provision for the flesh, to *fulfill its* lusts.

Romans 13

Please note that if your government are doing things that goes against God's commandments and moral laws, then you do not have to follow the government as you first have to be obedient to God,

Interpretation of my dream
Always remember that the enemy sends demons to stop and harass ministries. One of the main ways that he attacks is by stealing the life blood of the ministry which is its finance. The other is he brings impurity into the leadership. This is normally through sexual lust in one way or another and it can come through one person or even the whole leadership. Another way is he blinds the leadership to what is actually going on around them and then he can steal, kill and destroy whoever he wants, because the leadership is blind and cannot see.

My dream had all 3 of these elements. I prayed and asked God for a strategy on how to overcome this.

*Firstly, this man being in "**a deliverance ministry for 23 years**", knows full well that he cannot live with a woman that he is not married to. The Word of God tells us clearly to obey the laws of the land and the law states that man and woman should be married if they want to cohabitate and that the Church, Word of God and the Holy Spirit call this sin. The fact that he is not divorced even from his wife makes it even worse.*

Witchcraft in the Church

If he had divorced his wife and then married this other woman that he is with now, and if he asks God for forgiveness it will instantly put him back in right standing with God.

These two people live in an old yellow bus like the one I saw in the dream. The woman is very ill. She said that she has seen 3 visions of a monkey that is trying to look inside the bus. She rebuked the monkey every time.

This woman is oppressed by Incubus demon that causes her to be willing to stay in this lustful relationship and she might even have been sent by Satanists and demons to hold this man in captivity by causing him to sin sexually with her. She will see "monkeys" but they are actually demons and they are probably the ones that are controlling her and making her sick.

A couple of things have popped up since they joined us about two months ago. They have a couple of weird "things" that they believe in that I do not agree with. For instance they told one of our tenants, whom Chris and I were working with to get her saved for about 3 weeks that she does not need deliverance. This lady had some major generational curses and was cutting herself and a bunch of other "things" disturbing her. They told the lady she can do it herself and does not need us to do it. Yes she probably could if she knew how but she had no idea about Jesus or any of this.

This is because the demons that are operating on them are now controlling them. So any advice they give will be filtered through the demons rather than the Holy Spirit.

After some other incidents I told Tim that from the ministry side we should NOT ALLOW then to do ANYTHING in the church. Everything that they do and touch will be done via the demonic and not the Holy Spirit.

They also asked me (20 June 2012) if they can move in with us as they wanted to do "more" in the ministry and felt they could be more hands-on if they were with us 24/7. I found it very odd that only 6 days after I had renounced and cancelled this dream that they now wanted to move in with us.

The Holy Spirit told me not to allow this.

I have noticed that every time Tim posted something on his Facebook page or on one of the ministry pages that the lady would comment as if she "knows" better or was trying to make a statement that Tim did not put the correct posting.

Again the demonic will subvert everything that you try to do in the Holy Spirit

I strongly feel that this dream dealt with them and that they were trying to "worm" their way into my ministry to distract and mislead the congregation members. They are wolves in sheep clothing, either they repent and make right or they must leave. I asked them to leave the ministry and told them that when they are in right standing with God that they may return. They were very upset.

Since I have decided to work full time for God I have had numerous attacks and as well as had people sent on my way to distract or destroy something I was doing. God showed me that it is because of the enormous task that I have to do for Him and because I will be leading a huge number of people to Him and will help to save many souls.

I have also found that God is sending people with an anointing on them: Prophets, Evangelists, Teachers and Pastors, to me. People that are being held in bondage and that does not even know why some "things" are happening to them.

The knock

On 9 September 2011, Jacob left me. He started sleeping in the guest bedroom in our house. Two days after he left me at about 2am I heard a knock from under my bed. From under the tiles. I got such a fright.

The next morning I pulled the bed away and anointed the entire floor under the bed and asked God to close any entrances. For weeks I asked God to show me what or who was knocking from under the tiles under my bed.

Jacob returned and about 4 months later God said to me, at about 4:30am, "Listen". Suddenly Jacob's father knocked on our window and said he needs to stand up so that they can go to the gym. As they left God said listen again. I heard the knock on the window and just after that the knock on the tiles under my bed. I was shocked; it was exactly the same knock just on different surfaces.

A few weeks later I asked God to show me what Jacob is doing. I had a vision of what looked like the inside of a cave that was lit up by candles. I could see and hear everything. I saw a person on a rock with a flat surface.

Hélèné Fulton

The person was tied up. I saw many people around this person. I could recognize Jacob and his father. They were going to sacrifice this person on what looked like an altar. I felt the anger that they had towards this person. It was one of the scariest visions I have ever had.

Thereafter I had another vision of a man lizard (green as grass) drinking water from the river on our property. This man had a tail like a lizard and long nails.

I remember that before I had the fire of the Holy Spirit on my hands and feet I sometimes woke up due to something sharp hitting me on the soft side of the bottom of my foot. Almost like a sharp nail was hitting me there. It suddenly started to make sense.

I get many dreams and visions and I know that this is the way God speaks to us or warns us. I also know that this is the way that Satan attacks as it will always happen in the spiritual first before it manifests in the physical.

The table cloth

When I was still living in Durban I had a vision of a group of vampires gathering at a hall.

These vampires had normal teeth but a second set of razor sharp teeth came out of their gums. They also had dove grey wings about the size of a human's lungs. I recognized some of the faces in this group.
The man in charge was working at a local church.

We hired the church for our Sunday service in the afternoons.

Witchcraft in the Church

One Sunday a new congregation member, Anthony had an epileptic attack inside the church while I was doing the sermon. I just asked one of our prophets in our deliverance team to assist him and continue with the service as I knew Satan wanted the sermon to stop and I am not going to give him that satisfaction of stopping a service.

After the service I went to the man and sat next to him. He was doing extremely well as he was completely delivered from this demon.

While sitting and talking next to him I noticed that the table in front had a new table runner on. I was shocked to see the demon faces embroidered on this cloth.

I walked to the front to take a closer look and noticed that the entire table had small lice type insects on it.

This church also had a lot of candles in the church.

Satan controls the authority of the air

A demon named Temper causes you to have a temper.

A demon named depression causes you to be depressed.

Boyce and Boice are two demons that interfere with any electronic equipment, i.e., phone, computer, printer, automobile etc.

Hélèné Fulton

If something malfunctions, BIND UP these two demons, and command them to leave your equipment, in the name of Jesus.

Here is an incoming email received:

"Hi, Just thought I'd let you know it took me all these hours to run off your complete deliverance manual. My computer kept shutting down, the connection to the internet kept shutting off, I got signs coming up this is an illegal action, you probably have heard all this before, but the devil sure didn't want me to get hold of your material....I thought there has to be some good stuff in here if the devil is this mad.....as soon as I finished running if off, my computer is working perfect...not shutting down,....not getting unconnected. Praise Jesus, He's stronger than any devil. I had to keep taking authority over devils to get the manual printed, even the printer tried to jam up. What a praise report....really. Devil you loose!!! Praise the Lord. Thank you for your web site. Blessings"

On 28 March 2012. I spoke on my mobile with Jacob about his daughter being into witchcraft and that he needs to open his eyes and see what is going on around him. The person was crying and telling me that I am lying. 5 Minutes after the call ended all my software on my mobile was erased.

God gave me a revelation on…

[4] whose minds the god of this age has blinded, who do not believe, lest the light of the gospel of the glory of Christ, who is the image of God, should shine on them.

2 Corinthians 4:4

Witchcraft in the Church

Satan is called the god of this world or the age as per this Bible verse. The Greek word is Aion. The age means the dispensation we're in now.

> ²in which you once walked according to the course of this world, according to the prince of the power of the air, the spirit who now works in the sons of disobedience
>
> **Ephesians 2:2**

Satan is called the prince of the power of the air. Now the Greek word is Exousia which means authority. So Satan controls the authority of the air.

Satellites are in the air.

Internet signals are in the air.

Radio and Television signals are in the air.

Mobile phones especially text messaging is in the air.

No wonder Satan is controlling Television, Internet, Satellite and Mobile messages.

He is controlling it because he is the prince of authority of the air.

From a young age I had so many attacks on my life both spiritually and physically because of my calling.

I know now how to recognise the attacks, but it took me some serious training from the Holy Spirit.

Hélèné Fulton

You do not have to go through these attacks alone. At Light the World Ministries we send out teachings daily and we stand together in prayer. Although Light the World Ministries has home based churches (we do it Jesus style), we are an online ministry that is available through E-mail, Black Berry Messenger, WeChat & Whatsup in order to assist our members.

Chapter 11: Cursed Objects and Hosts

If you have a cursed object, you become cursed! Remove all cursed objects from your being and from your home; destroy by burning them. Do not keep the cursed silver or gold of the object.

If you move into a new house anoint the house.

I was asked to come and "clean" a house on the Bluff in Durban.

The couple that stayed there were experiencing a couple of weird things. They could feel a presence in the house. The lady said that almost every day she would find human [13]fecus inside her cupboards. They would find urine on the floors and on the tables.

Their belongings would disappear from a locked home.

I anointed the house and got the family born again after I explained to them what it means.

Please email us on (churchoffice@lighttheworldminsitries.co.za) for a teaching on how to prepare and pray over anointing oil and how to anoint your house according to what the Holy Spirit has shown me to also get rid of water spirits.

Cursed objects are any objects used in any occultic rituals or that has been dedicated to demons (idols,

---

[13] Human Bowel movement from the anus

artefact's, etc.) The best course of action is to destroy them. However, it is well to check second-hand cars, homes and apartments also because if the former owners had Ouija boards, or other occult paraphernalia, or were involved in serious bondage to sin, then there is every reason to suspect that evil spirits could be lingering behind. These spirits can and will cause trouble to the new owners.

When burning the object, please ensure that you are in a place where no other people are around. Make sure to send the demons back to the dark kingdom.

I see the latest craze among the young people is to put a gemstone between their eyes. This is a Hindu practice for the third eye. You are opening yourself up to a number of evil spirits.

Young people also like to wear a bracelet on the top part of their arms. Sometimes even a snake type bracelet. This is a pagan tradition.

Candles

Sometimes people have no electricity and have to use candles. I urge you to rather change to oil lamps as soon as possible.

On our deliverance website, we talk about objects in your home that can be "hosts" for demons. Candles can also be a "host".

A former African witchdoctor who practiced witchcraft for over twenty years said that demons are attracted to the substance candles are made of. He used candles as part of his witchcraft.

Witchcraft in the Church

Candles are used in satanic rituals as well as in other pagan religions.

Colour, shape, or smell does not matter. When lit, the smell of the candle also calls on another big time demon. No wonder the candle business is bringing in billions of dollars a year!

Many churches have candles all over the place. I often wonder why the pastor of the church allows candles in the church, so I took it to the Father in prayer and He told me this: "My child those pastors do not have discernment, they do not spend enough time studying and most of them are doing witchcraft when they think no one sees them. They forget that I see them all the time."

Get rid of all your candles. You may just be getting rid of some of your problems. This also pertains to incense.

[17] But we will certainly do whatever has gone out of our own mouth, to burn incense to the queen of heaven and pour out drink offerings to her, as we have done, we and our fathers, our kings and our princes, in the cities of Judah and in the streets of Jerusalem. For *then* we had plenty of food, were well-off, and saw no trouble. [18] But since we stopped burning incense to the queen of heaven and pouring out drink offerings to her, we have lacked everything and have been consumed by the sword and by famine."
[19] *The women also said,* "And when we burned incense to the queen of heaven and poured out drink offerings to her, did we make cakes for her, to worship her, and pour out drink offerings to her without our husbands' *permission?*"

Hélèné Fulton

[20] Then Jeremiah spoke to all the people—the men, the women, and all the people who had given him *that* answer—saying: [21] "The incense that you burned in the cities of Judah and in the streets of Jerusalem, you and your fathers, your kings and your princes, and the people of the land, did not the LORD remember them, and did it *not* come into His mind? [22] So the LORD could no longer bear *it,* because of the evil of your doings *and* because of the abominations which you committed. Therefore your land is a desolation, an astonishment, a curse, and without an inhabitant, as *it is* this day. [23] Because you have burned incense and because you have sinned against the LORD, and have not obeyed the voice of the LORD or walked in His law, in His statutes or in His testimonies, therefore this calamity has happened to you, as *at* this day."

[24] Moreover Jeremiah said to all the people and to all the women, "Hear the word of the LORD, all Judah who *are* in the land of Egypt! [25] Thus says the LORD of hosts, the God of Israel, saying: 'You and your wives have spoken with your mouths and fulfilled with your hands, saying, "We will surely keep our vows that we have made, to burn incense to the queen of heaven and pour out drink offerings to her." You will surely keep your vows and perform your vows!' [26] Therefore hear the word of the LORD, all Judah who dwell in the land of Egypt: 'Behold, I have sworn by My great name,' says the LORD, 'that My name shall no more be named in the mouth of any man of Judah in all the land of Egypt, saying, "The Lord GOD lives."

Jeremiah 44:17-26

For those Bible researchers who read that "candles" were mentioned in the Bible, look in your Strong's concordance. The Original term is "lamp" "oil" or "oil lamp", NOT "candle". The menorah tradition goes back to 165 B.C. They did not use candles, but used oil.

After you get rid of the candles, command all the demons to leave you and your property, in the name of Jesus, JUST IN CASE.

Witchcraft in the Church

What if the lights go out, you say? Use a flashlight or battery operated emergency lights!

Looking at it on the basis of your health, this article was in the August 2000 issue of Better Homes and Gardens magazine under Health Update:

"Are your candles making you sick?

You love the warm glow and calming scents of your favourite candles. But you probably won't be as enamoured of the prospect that these same candles may be emitting lead particles into your home.

"The last thing people would imagine is that candles can be little lead smelters," says Sidney Wolfe, the director of Public Citizen's Health Research Group in Washington D.C.

The group examined 285 candles from twelve different stores in the D.C. area. Eighty-six had metal wicks, and laboratory tests found that nine had wicks containing high amounts of lead.

The group says burning a lead-wicked candle for three hours can cause lead levels in the air to be nine to 33 times higher than federal safety standards. Airborne lead can be inhaled or it can settle on surfaces, where it can be ingested.

Wolfe urges people to check their candles for metal wicks. You can tell by looking straight down at the wick to see if there is a metal tip in the centre. Not all metal

wicks contain lead, but to be on the safe side, don't burn any candles with metal wicks.
Lead poisoning may damage the central nervous system and cause abnormal development and behaviour and learning problems in children."

The following is part of an article that was in THE CLARION-LEDGER from Jackson, Mississippi on December 20, 1998.

Wax facts - Retail sales of candles are fast approaching $2 Billion annually in the United States, a 15% increase since the early 1990's. Candle sales during the holidays is 35%, and 65% during non-holidays.

Each of the nation's 50 major candle manufacturers can make 1,000 to 2,000 different varieties of candles, encompassing different colours, shapes, sizes or scents, according to the National Candle Association. And these days, it's the smell that sells.

They even have candles that smell like food - chocolate, honeydew, grapefruit, fig.

The following is part of an article that was in THE CLARION-LEDGER from Jackson, Mississippi on December 29, 1997.

The National Candle Association reports sales of candles up 25% in the past five years. In 1997, more than 4 billion candles will be sold in the United States. "Candles have become a huge trend," says a local store owner. "People are going nuts over them -- every size, shape and scent you can think of." "We have 300 or 400 candles fly out of here every day," says another store owner. "People want the big ones, the little ones, the tall ones, the tall skinny ones, the short skinny ones, candles that burn a certain colour, candles that give off a certain fragrance...man, its serious business."

Candles have been around a long time -- they were used in Egypt and Crete as early at 3000 B.C., and by the 13th century candles were being manufactured by craftsmen. But just recently candles have become big business. They have candle parties just like Tupperware parties. "I was amazed and surprised by the volume sold (with only about a dozen people at the party). Some people spent more than $100."

One woman says, "There's just so many things you can do with candles. You can decorate. You can actually use them to take you back to your childhood, to recapture a smell of something, maybe a gardenia. Or you can use them just to relax. I'll burn candles everywhere, and it's extremely relaxing to me."

"In the last four or five years, we've seen steady growth in the industry. I think a big part of it is decorative, simply because you can change the whole look of a room simply by adding candles. But I think another part of it is something called aromatherapy, which a lot of people are getting into." Aromatherapy contends that scents can enhance a person's mood.

"No doubt it works. For instance, a lavender candle is anti-stress. I've had people tell me that they'd had trouble sleeping, then burned a lavender candle just before going to bed. They said they slept like a baby."

And, there are dozens of other candle specialties. Some are dripless and smokeless. "This is a big deal for weddings and things like that." Some are odour eaters.

Hélèné Fulton

*"They contain chlorophyll, and it eliminates the smell of smoke, pets and food." Some serve as a decongestant.
"We have one that's called a eucalyptus. A lot of parents buy them to put in the room of a child who has asthma or a cold. The effect is amazing, really."*

And the good thing about candles is that you can spend what you want -- from less than $1 to hundreds of dollars. "We got some candles in a couple of weeks ago that sold for between $80 and $100. They were gone in no time. They were a 5-by-12, natural-colour candle with some sculptures of grapes on them. They were really unusual, and usually those sell pretty quickly."

During 2011 a lady that stayed closed to us gave my grandson a white candle. He was so pleased. After taking this to God in prayer I was shown that this woman was linking into his innocence and purity. I do not normally do this but I want to point out the fact that most candles that you buy for household purposes are white. I was told by a former witch how they went to candle factories in the spirit and chant on the production line for doors to be opened for them to the houses that use the candles and how they place curses on the candles

In witchcraft a white candle can also replace any other colour if you do not have that colour. Scary!!! Definitely!

*The statement below comes from a witch's mouth:
In witchcraft burning a white candle is used to summoning spirit guides (demons), performing astral travel, and to enhance psychic abilities during divination. What people do not know is that depending on the colour of candle we can cause illness and steal prosperity or love.*

Witchcraft in the Church

I think I made it very clear that candles should not be used in your house. Now you ask me what do I if I cannot afford to change to oil lamps. Try and buy at least one lamp a month. While doing this do not buy any new candles. Pray and seal the candles with the blood of Jesus Christ. Also if you are using the candles when you have no electricity ask God to place a legion of warrior angels around your house to protect it from any evil trying to enter the house. Remember you cannot do this if you are trying to get away with keeping your candles for decorative or other purposes than using it for light, if you cannot afford to change to oil lamps immediately.

THE DEVIL HAS A CANDLE FOR EVERY NEED. HE MAKES IT LOOK GOOD AND SMELL GOOD JUST SO YOU CAN BRING HIS DEMONS INTO YOUR HOME.

List of cursed objects and practices to avoid.

Please note that there are many other cursed objects and you should ask the Holy Spirit to always guide you before you buy or accept and item.

So many people today bring into their homes things (clothing, food, interior-design, statues, photographs, books, music, games, souvenirs ...) with connections to the occult, paganism and all kinds of spirits.

Please be very discerning about what you bring in your house.

Aliens: Demonic activity

Hélèné Fulton

Astrology/Horoscopes: Astrology has its roots in ancient paganism and the study and seeking of answers in the stars.

Buddhism Images
Do not even touch a Buddha statue as this will bring a curse on you.

Crystal Balls: Mediums/Occult

Chain Letters: Any form of letter telling you to forward to others for luck or blessings ect.

Charms: Pagan Origins, first originated by Egyptians for warding off evil spirits.

Dungeons & Dragons: Role playing gaming

Dream catchers

Egyptian gods, Egyptian Mythology, Pyramids: Occult connections, Eye of Horus found on many popular rock and roll albums now, also found on many internet games.

Freemason Symbols: Secret society

Fairies: Occult ties, associated to Wiccan/Witchcraft. Fairies are generally described as human in appearance and having magical powers.

Fortune Telling, Psychics, Mediums, Tea Leaves

Greek gods/Mythology: Ancient Paganism

All Halloween Objects & Everything to do with

Witchcraft in the Church

Hindu Images & Jewellery

Islamic Symbols

Labyrinth/Mazes: Pagan Origin, Greek Mythology. They have historically been used both in group ritual and for private meditation.

Martial Arts: Pagan Origins, the term is ultimately derived from Latin, martial arts being the "Arts of Mars," the Roman god of war. Martial arts can also be linked with religion and spirituality. Numerous systems are reputed to have been founded, disseminated, or practiced by monks or nuns. For example gatka is a weapon-based Indian martial art created by the Sikhs of the Panjab region of India and the Kshatriya caste of Hindus also have an ancient martial art named Shastravidhya. Japanese styles, when concerning non-physical qualities of the combat, are strongly influenced by Zen philosophy.

Mermaids: Ancient Greek Mythology paganism

The first known mermaid stories appeared in Assyria, ca. 1000 BC. The goddess Atargatis, mother of Assyrian queen Semiramis, loved a mortal shepherd and unintentionally killed him. Ashamed, she jumped into a lake to take the form of a fish, but the waters would not conceal her divine beauty. Thereafter, she took the form of a mermaid—human above the waist, fish below—though the earliest representations of Atargatis showed her as a fish with a human head and legs, similar to the Babylonian Era. The Greeks recognized Atargatis under the name Derketo. Prior to 546 BC, the Milesian philosopher Anaximander proposed that mankind had sprung from an aquatic species of animal. He thought that humans, with their extended infancy, could not have survived otherwise. (the Starbucks logo)

Ninja: Pagan Origins
Ninja figure prominently in folklore and legend, and as a result it is often difficult to separate historical fact from myth. Some legendary abilities include invisibility, walking on water and control over natural elements. The ninja emerged as mercenaries in the 15th century, where they were recruited as spies, raiders, arsonists and even terrorists. Amongst the samurai, a sense of ritual and decorum was observed, where one was expected to fight or duel openly. Combined with the unrest of the Sengoku era, these factors created a demand for men willing to commit deeds considered not respectable for conventional warriors.

Ouija Board: Occult connections

Oriental Pagan Religious Symbols: Ying Yang for example

Pagan gods: Any god(s) worshipped by any pagan religion

Pokemon Cards: Occult / Witchcraft for children

Roman gods: Ancient Paganism, Roman Mythology

Science Fiction: Oriented to promoting or looking into futures that don't include God's Plans. Only God's Plans are true, do not focus on the vain imaginations of men who do not seek to trust in God exclusively and contrive and fantasize over their own vain imaging's of what the future might be.

Witchcraft in the Church

Statues of men/animals/Catholic saints and other statues to worship

Tarot Cards

Vampires

Voodoo: Occult origins

Witches/Witchcraft/Wiccan/Wizards

Wind chimes: Occult/Wiccan/Pagan background

Yin and Yang Symbol: Pagan Symbol

Yoga: Originated in India through pagan religion. The goal of yoga, or of the person practicing yoga, is the attainment of a state of perfect spiritual insight and tranquillity. The word is associated with meditative practices in Hinduism, Buddhism and Jainism.

² And Jacob said to his household and to all who *were* with him, "Put away the foreign gods that *are* among you, purify yourselves, and change your garments.

Genesis 35:2

¹³ So Saul died for his unfaithfulness which he had committed against the LORD, because he did not keep the word of the LORD, and also because he consulted a medium for guidance.

1 Chronicles 10:13

¹⁸ and say, 'Thus says the Lord GOD: "Woe to the *women* who sew *magic* charms on their sleeves and make veils for the heads of

people of every height to hunt souls! Will you hunt the souls of My people, and keep yourselves alive?

Ezekiel 13:18

² And Jacob said to his household and to all who *were* with him, "Put away the foreign gods that *are* among you, purify yourselves, and change your garments.

Genesis 35:2

³¹ 'Give no regard to mediums and familiar spirits; do not seek after them, to be defiled by them: I *am* the LORD your God.

Leviticus 19:31

¹⁵ "Take careful heed to yourselves, for you saw no form when the LORD spoke to you at Horeb out of the midst of the fire, ¹⁶ lest you act corruptly and make for yourselves a carved image in the form of any figure: the likeness of male or female, ¹⁷ the likeness of any animal that *is* on the earth or the likeness of any winged bird that flies in the air, ¹⁸ the likeness of anything that creeps on the ground or the likeness of any fish that *is* in the water beneath the earth.

Deuteronomy 4:15-18

⁴ "You shall not make for yourself a carved image—any likeness *of anything* that *is* in heaven above, or that *is* in the earth beneath, or that *is* in the water under the earth;

Exodus 20:4

²⁶ 'You shall not make idols for yourselves;
neither a carved image nor a sacred pillar shall you rear up for yourselves;
nor shall you set up an engraved stone in your land, to bow down to it;
for I am the Lord your God.

Leviticus 26:1

⁶ 'And the person who turns to mediums and familiar spirits, to

Witchcraft in the Church

prostitute himself with them, I will set My face against that person and cut him off from his people.

Leviticus 20:6

[10] There shall not be found among you *anyone* who makes his son or his daughter pass through the fire, *or one* who practices witchcraft, *or* a soothsayer, or one who interprets omens, or a sorcerer

Deuteronomy 18:10

[6] Also he caused his sons to pass through the fire in the Valley of the Son of Hinnom; he practiced soothsaying, used witchcraft and sorcery, and consulted mediums and spiritists. He did much evil in the sight of the Lord, to provoke Him to anger.

2 Chronicles 33:6

While I was married to Jacob, he gave me 4 presents in the beginning of our marriage. These were all jewellery.

The minute I wear them I had the following symptoms:

Tiredness
Forgetfulness
My voice became hoarse
I felt depressed
I battled to read the Bible and pray

Satanic Signs and Symbols

Do not buy clothes, jewellery or anything else with these signs on. Also make sure that the hand signs you use are not satanic.

Hélèné Fulton

3 weeks ago I was watching a daily South African soap, and one of the young actresses was wearing a T-Shirt with the Cross of Nero on it. Purely a lack of knowledge. 6 months ago my sister and her family were under severe spiritual attack and I asked God to show me what was wrong. God showed me the Cross of Nero. I started asking her children who had something like this, no one had and then coming out of my sisters bathroom I saw a necklace hanging over the side of her dressing table only the chain was visible.

It was the cross of Nero. Her husband bought this for her almost 9 months ago and she never wore it but hung it on the dressing table and forgot about it. Well Satan never forgets about anything. Satan likes to accuse you daily in front of God and this necklace gave him the legal right to do so.

Witchcraft in the Church

Inverted Pentagram Symbolizes the morning star, a name Satan has taken. Used in witchcraft and occult rituals to conjure up evil spirits. Satanists use it 2 points up and pagans use it one point up. Any way it is used symbolizes evil. It matters not if two points are up or one. It matters not if it has a circle around it. It still is a symbol of Satan.

Baphomet Unique to Satanism. A demonic deity and symbolic of Satan. Can be seen as jewelry.
It is also now being used by the masons. It can be seen on their buildings and the emblems they put on their vehicles to identify each other.

Hélèné Fulton

Pentagram - Symbol used in Witchcraft. It represents the elements, earth, wind, fire and water with the spirit surrounding them.

Hexagram - It is one of the most potent symbols used in the working of the powers of darkness. Used to work magic.

I get a lot of mails on this one. Satanism takes and perverts Christian symbols. It is satanic when used in an Occult setting with a circle around it.

Witchcraft in the Church

Ankh - Symbolizes fertility rites and the building up of lust within a person. A spirit of Lust is the power of this union of male /female representations. Also called the Long Life Seal.

Swastika or Sun Wheel - An ancient religious symbol used long before Hitler came to power. It was used in Buddhist inscriptions, Celtic monuments and Greek coins. In sun god worship, it is supposed to represent the sun's course in the heavens.

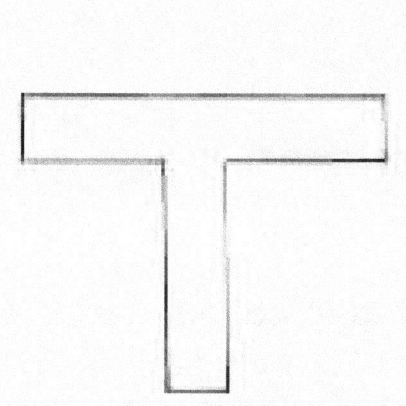

Tau Cross - Symbol of the god Mathras of the Persians and the Aryans of India. To them, Mathras was an "angel of light" or the "heavenly light". It is used in modern Masonry under the symbol of the T square.

Italian Horn - Other names....Unicorn horn and Leprechaun staff. Introduced by the Lord Druids of Scotland and Ireland. It is associated with good luck and good fortune. It is also used to ward off "Maluka" or the "Evil Eye". It also means Satan will take care of your finances.

Witchcraft in the Church

All Seeing Eye - Believed to be the eye of Lucifer and those who claim control of it have control of world finances. Used in divination. Hexes, curses, psychic control and all corruption are worked through this emblem. This one is a symbol of the Illuminati. Look at U.S. currency.

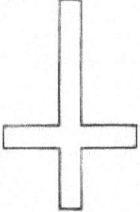

Upside Down Cross - Symbolizes mockery and rejection of Jesus. Necklaces are worn by many Satanists'. It can be seen on Rock singers and their album covers.

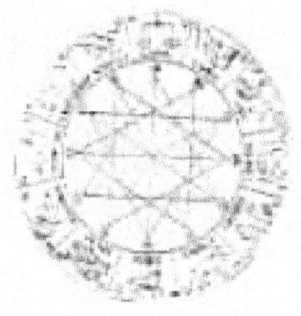

Héléné Fulton

Zodiac - Used in satanic and occult worship. Practitioners are acknowledging their god as Baal or Lucifer. Horoscope signs are included

Goat Head - The horned goat, goat of mendes, Baphomet, god of the witches, the scapegoat. It's a Satanists way of mocking Jesus as the "Lamb" who died for our sins.

Cross of Nero - Or Peace sign. Another sign that mocks the cross of Jesus. Also known as "The Dead Man Rune". It appears on the tombstones of some of Hitler's SS troops.

Yin-Yang - In Chinese philosophy, two great opposite principles or forces on whose interplay everything depends.

Witchcraft in the Church

Yang is male, light and positive; Yin is female, dark and negative.

Scarab Beetle - The dung beetle which is the Egyptian symbol of reincarnation. It is also a symbol of Beelzebub, Lord of the flies (Satan). It is worn by occultists to show that they have power and is a source of protection.

Satanic "S"

Satanic "S" - Represents a lightning bolt that means "Destroyer". In mythology, It was the weapon of Zeus. Worn to have power over others. Also was worn by the feared SS of Nazi Germany.

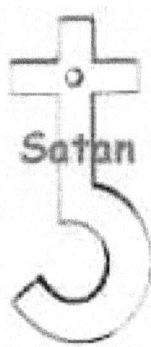

Satanic Cross - Upside down question mark that questions the Deity of God. Within the occult it is the representation of the three crown princes; Satan, Belial and leviathan. Symbolizes complete power under Lucifer.

Udjat - or all seeing eye. Also know as "the eye of ra". One of few symbols referring to Lucifer (king of hell), whom it is though will pass judgment. Below the eye is a tear because he mourns for those outside his influence.

Star and Crescent - Represents the moon goddess Dianna and the "son of the morning", the name of Lucifer in Isaiah 14:12.

Witchcraft in the Church

Witchcraft uses it the way shown and Satanism turns it in the opposite direction.

Anarchy - Means to abolish all laws. In other words "do what thou wilt" the law of Satanists. Used by Punk rockers and Heavy Metal followers.

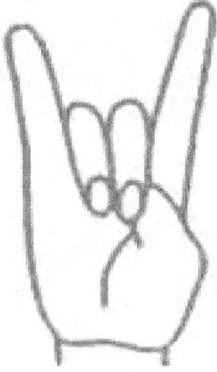

Horned God Represents the horned god of witchcraft. Pan or Cernunnos. Note the thumb under the fingers and given by the right hand.

Horned Hand - The sign of recognition between those in the Occult. When pointed at someone it is meant to place a curse. Note the thumb over the fingers and given by the left hand.

Witch Sign or Moon Sign **Used to salute the rising moon.** Used by surfers and football teams due to a lack of knowledge.

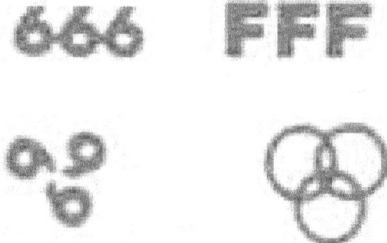

666 -The number of man. The mark of the Beast as described in Revelation.

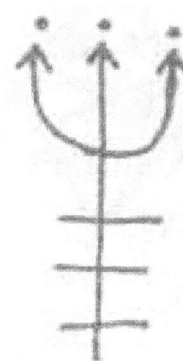

Bad Company Tied to the temple of Psychic Youth.

Witchcraft in the Church

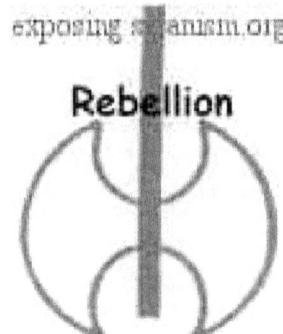

Anti Justice - The roman symbol for justice was an axe upright.
Being upside-down it represents anti justice or rebellion.
Feminists use a double axe upright as a symbol of ancient matriarchy.

Black Mass Indicator - Indicates a black mass has or will take place. It mocks the catholic mass. Holy Items are defiled and the Lord's prayer is recited backwards.

Church of Satan Founded by Anton LaVey in 1966.

Hélèné Fulton

Holy Earth Symbol for mother earth. Also appears as a Hopi medicine wheel and Norse sun symbol.

Seal of the Left Hand Path - Indicates Black magic and the path to Satan.

Labyrinth - A maze design of bronze age Crete that symbolizes the path of initiation.

Witchcraft in the Church

Spiral - Ancient Goddess symbol of universal pattern of growth in nature. A variation with three lines was used by some to represent the number of the beast.. 666

Blood Ritual Symbol - Represents animal and human sacrifices.

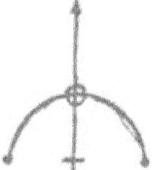

Sexual Ritual Symbol - Used to indicate the place and purpose.

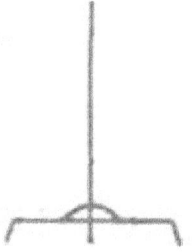

Inverted Cross of Satanic Justice If found carved in the chest of a victim, it means the person was a traitor. The vertical line represents man's presence. The horizontal line indicates eternity past and future. The arch represents the world and being inverted is mockery of God.

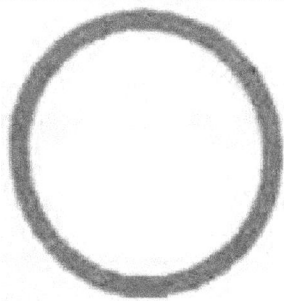

Ritual Circle - Has different meanings to different groups. Protection from evil, symbolic of life cycles or completeness. Nine feet across with a smaller one inside and perhaps a pentagram drawn inside.

Sword of Power - May be seen upright or upside down with a drop of blood. Used by some Satanists to represent light and darkness.

Talisman or Amulet - Believed to have magical powers. Usually has a drawing or writing with the name or image of a deity.

Trident - Symbol of enforcement among occult groups. There are many variations.

Witchcraft in the Church

Thaumaturgic Triangle - Used for magical purposes in casting of spells and the summoning of demons. Found near ritual sites. Believed to be the door through which the demon will be called.

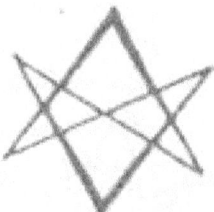

Unincursive Hexagram - Designed by Aleister Crowley as the symbol of his Order of the Silver Star, Astrum Argentum or AA

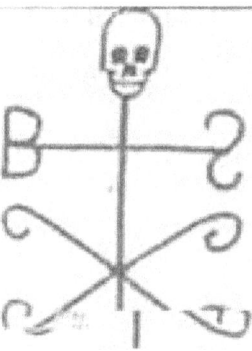

Veve - Designs used in Voudoun to summon the various Loa or spirit deities. Symbol for Baron Samadi, Lord of the graveyard and death.

Many of these satanic symbols are in online games. I have also seen some of these signs being used in a well know clothing retail store. Please do not let your children wear these signs.

Hélèné Fulton

For more signs and symbols visit
http://www.radioliberty.com/Symbolsandtheirmeaning.html

[14]The P.O.D Symbol

SOME EXAMPLES OF THE P.O.D. SYMBOL

P.O.D. "Warriors" Album
Symbol in Top Right

From P.O.D.'s website
(www.payableondeath.com)

P.O.D. Patch
Symbol in middle of
"O"

On P.O.D.'s website (www.thesouthtown.com) under the section "Frequently Asked Questions", someone asks about the "trinity symbol"?

What does the trinity symbol mean?
The symbol is known as a 'triquetra' that is derived from ancient Celtic knotwork & adopted by Christians around St. Patrick's time as a symbol of the Trinity (Father, Son, & Holy Spirit). The interweaving lines represent One being in Three separate, but equal parts.
(http://www.thesouthtown.com/faq/#6)

---

[14] The P.O.D information was given with permission from Dial-the-Truth Ministries, Dr. Terry Watkins, Th.D. (http://www.av1611.org/crock/pod_sym.html)

Witchcraft in the Church

But there's one problem with representing the Trinity, or the Godhead with symbols — **it's CLEARY FORBIDDEN in the Bible!**

Acts 17:29, clearly FORBIDS such symbology: ". . . we ought NOT to think that **the Godhead** [the Trinity] is like unto gold, or silver, or stone, **GRAVEN BY ART** [symbols, icons, etc.] and man's device."

That could NOT POSSIBLY be any clearer!

To represent the Trinity or God as a "symbol" or "image", etc. is strictly forbidden. All throughout the Old Testament the use of graven images are strictly forbidden! **The very FIRST of the ten commandments forbids such symbolism!**

3 "You shall have no other gods before Me.
4 "**You shall not make for yourself a carved image—any likeness of anything that is in heaven above, or that is in the earth beneath, or that is in the water under the earth;**

Exodus 20:3-4

There are many other verses in both the Old and New Testament against the use of symbols, images, etc. to represent God or any false god.

Not surprising, since symbols are strictly forbidden by the Lord God, symbols are highly esteemed in witchcraft and the occult.

Hélèné Fulton

Harpers' Encyclopedia of Mystical & Paranormal Experience (p.594) says, **"Symbols are important to all esoteric teachings**, for they contain secret wisdom accessible only to the initiated."
(Harpers' Encyclopedia of Mystical & Paranormal Experience, p.594)

It's also worth noting the symbol used by P.O.D. is also on the cover of the New King James Bible. The New Spirit filled King James Bible does not have this symbol.

The Aquarian Conspiracy, a key New Age "handbook", bears a similar symbol. And New Agers freely admit it represents three inter-woven "6"s or "666".

Constance Cumbey, author of The Hidden Dangers of the Rainbow and a notable authority on the New Age Movement, says concerning the symbol:

"On the cover of the Aquarian Conspiracy is a Mobius, it is really used by them as triple six (666). The emblem on the cover of the New King James Bible **(same symbol as**

P.O.D.'s) is said to be an ancient symbol of the Trinity. The old symbol had gnostic origins. It was more gnostic than Christian. **I was rather alarmed when I noticed the emblem..."**
(The New Age Movement, Southwest Radio Church, 1982 p.11)

ABOVE: The three esoteric "6"'s separated. Plainly displaying the interlocked "666".

The Institute of Transpersonal Psychology

The Triqueta is used as the centerpiece for the logo for The Institute of Transpersonal Psychology (ITP). The ITP is a new age school following the Jungian Psychology (occultist Carl Jung). One of their stated goals is ". . . to reach the recognition of divinity within" (www.itp.edu/about/tp.html) (see Genesis 3:5, "...ye shall be as gods...")

Hélèné Fulton

The same symbol (with a circle as does P.O.D. also) is displayed by the rock group Led Zeppelin. Members of Led Zeppelin are deeply involved in satanism and the occult. Guitarist Jimmy Page, so consumed with satanism, actually purchased satanist Aleister Crowley's mansion. Most believe the symbol is from the teachings of Aleister Crowley and represents 666.

LED ZEPPELIN LOGO

The Hierophant

ABOVE: The picture is "The Hierophant" taken from the Tarot card set designed by Satanist, Aliester Crowley. The "Hierophant" is a priest in the occult and Eleusinian. Notice the "three circles" at the top of the wand or rod in the Hierphant's hand. Inside the three intertwined circles is the "P.O.D. symbol".

RIGHT: To the right is the top of the wand enlarged. Notice the "P.O.D. symbol" (upside down) inside the three circles.
One of the most occult television shows ever aired is "Charmed". "Charmed"

from the "Charmed" TV series

Witchcraft in the Church

details the spells and occultic practices of three witches.

The "P.O.D. symbol" is the show's primary symbol of witchcraft and is splattered throughout the series. Notice the "P.O.D. symbol" displayed on "The Book of Shadows". The Book of Shadows is commonly used in witchcraft and satanism:

Book of Shadows: Also called a grimoire, this journal kept either by individual witches or satanists or by a coven or group, records the activities of the group and the incantations used. (Jerry Johnston, The Edge of Evil: The Rise of Satanism on North America, p. 269)

	THE P.O.D. SYMBOL & WITCHCRAFT? **The Craft: A Witch's Book of Shadows** The Witch's Book of Shadows or Grimoire is a book of spells, enchantments, and rituals. Includes Rituals, Spells, and Wicca Ethics **The Craft Companion: A Witch's Journal** By Dorothy Morrison, a high priest of Witchcraft. **NOTE: We circled in, and also enlarged to the side The P.O.D. symbol.**	

Hélèné Fulton

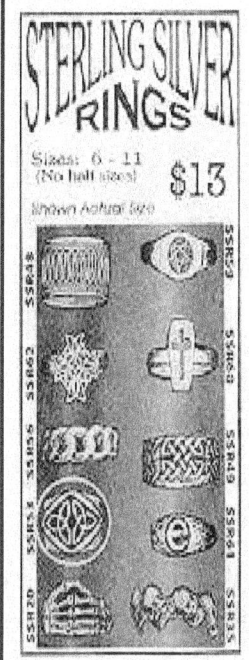

Here's some examples of Satanic and Pagan Jewelry which includes the P.O.D. symbol.
LEFT BOX: Notice the satanic pentagram ring in the top right corner. The ring with the P.O.D. symbol is the fourth down on the left, we highlighted it with a yellow circle.
BOTTOM BOX: Notice the very satanic Baphomet Goat.
We broke out and colored the P.O.D. symbol found in the other two satanic pieces of jewellery.

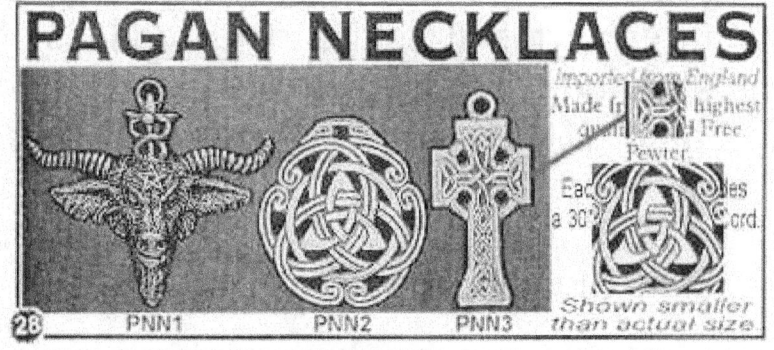

ABOVE: The image on the left is from the rock group Deicide's album "Once Upon the Cross". It is a triquetra (NOTICE: Also like Led Zeppelin, Charmed and P.O.D. it is enclosed within a circle) with pentagrams and upside down crosses. The group Deicide members are very serious Satanists. Lead Singer Glen Benton has an upside down cross branded on his forehead. The inside covers of the album "Once Upon the Cross" has the Lord Jesus Christ, sliced up the middle, with his insides removed. The name Deicide means the death of God.

The book "Blood on the Doorposts" by former Satanists, Bill and Sharon Schnoebelen, also documents the "trio of sixes (666)" in the "P.O.D. & NKJV symbol" and goes so far as claim it is "symbolic of the anti-christ":

"A disguised interlocked trio of sixes, symbolic of the anti-christ. Also symbolizes the triple goddess of Wicca (three interlocked vesica pisces together). Commonly used in Catholic liturgical iconography, **and has recently found its way into the logo of the New King James Bible** [also P.O.D.'s symbol]." (Bill and Sharon Schnoebelen, Blood on the Doorposts, p. 150)

Dr. Cathy Burns, probably the world's leading authority on occult symbols, writes in her book, Masonic and Occult Symbols Illustrated, concerning the "P.O.D. symbol":

"Marilyn Ferguson, a New Ager, used the symbol of the triquetra (another name for the triskele) on her book The Aquarian Conspiracy. **This is a variation for the number 666**. Other books and material have a similar design printed on them, such as books from David Spangler, the person who lauds Lucifer, and The Witch's Grimoire. As most people know, the number 666 is the number of the beast (see Revelation 13:18) and is evil, yet the occultists and New Agers love this number and consider it to be sacred.

As stated earlier, many organizations, such as the World Future Society and the Trilateral Commission, incorporate this symbol into their logo. **I think it is quite interesting to see that this same symbol appears on the cover of the New King James Bible as well**! (as it also does on P.O.D.s albums, web site, shirts, etc.)"
(Dr. Cathy Burns, Masonic and Occult Symbols Illustrated, pp. 242-243)

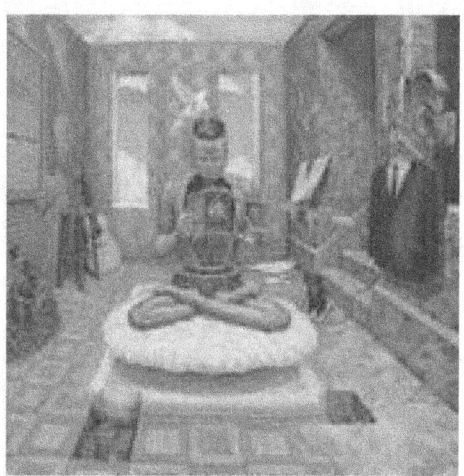

Fundamental Elements of Southtown

The cover of P.O.D.s platinum selling album *The Fundamental Elements of Southtown* is covered with occult symbols. Notice the man sitting in the occult "lotus" position. The occult initiate believes the "lotus" position connects to the spiritual transcendence of oneness with god. *Harpers' Encyclopedia of Mystical & Paranormal Experience* writes of the "lotus" position: **"The most common sitting posture used in yoga and other forms of meditation. The position facilitates the flow of the universal life force through the top of the head and into the chakras."** (*Harpers' Encyclopedia of Mystical & Paranormal Experience*, p. 332)

P.O.D. clearly understand the spiritual significance of the lotus position, as the man is levitating on a cloud. Of course, the practice of levitation is a well known occult practice. *Harpers' Encyclopedia of Mystical & Paranormal Experience* writes, **"Levitations are said to occur in mediumship, shamanistic trance, mystical rapture and trance,**

magic, bewitchment, hauntings, and possession." (*Harpers' Encyclopedia of Mystical & Paranormal Experience*, p. 327)

The Dictionary of Cults, Sects, Religions and the Occult, classifies "levitation" as **"occult; spiritualism and voodoo"** (Mather, George A. and Larry Nichols, *The Dictionary of Cults, Sects, Religions and the Occult*, p. 175)

There are many other occult images on the cover of *The Fundamental Elements of Southtown* album. In fact, because of the blatant occult influences covering *The Fundamental Elements of Southtown* album, many Christian bookstores totally banned the album.

There are many other occult influences on the cover of *The Fundamental Elements of Southtown* album. In fact, because of the occult influences covering *The Fundamental Elements of Southtown* album, many Christian bookstores totally banned the album.

But, as they say, "you ain't seen nothing yet"!

If the Christian bookstores were shocked by the occult symbols decorating *The Fundamental Elements of*

Hélèné Fulton

Southtown, the occult artistry of P.O.D.'s 2003 release, *Payable on Death* should (and did!) send them into spiritual cardiac arrest!

In over 25 years of researching occult influences in rock music, P.O.D.s album *Payable on Death* artwork is clearly among the most openly occult and dark I have ever seen. The fact that P.O.D. plastered such artwork throughout their CD insert unmistakably reveals a very serious spiritual condition. **This occult artwork should not be taken lightly. P.O.D. is a spiritually confused band that Christian young people should avoid at all cost.** Young person, please pay careful and prayerful attention to what you are about to read. Also, the following analysis may appear lengthy and comprehensive, but the truth is, comparable to the amount of occult images found, it is brief.

P.O.D.'s album cover **(ABOVE)** displays a semi-nude woman (with her crossed arms covering her bare breasts) wearing a crown with the wings of a butterfly. The winged-lady-butterfly is a mystic fairy. Fairies have a long and winding history in witchcraft and the occult. *The Woman's Dictionary of Symbols and Sacred Objects* describes the fairy as, **"tiny female spirit with butterfly wings. . ."** (p. 246) **The fairy is depicted as a Queen with a crown.** (p. 245) It goes on to say, ". . . the fairies were originally the souls of the pagan dead. . . In several folk ballads the **Fairy Queen** is addressed as 'Queen of Heaven'. . . Christian sources depicted fairies as real people, **almost synonymous with witches**." (*The Woman's Dictionary of Symbols and Sacred Objects,* p. 246)

The *Guide to the Occult and Mysticism* writes of fairies:

"According to theory, fairies are either: earthbound unbaptized souls; guardians of the souls of the dead; ghosts of venerated ancestors; **fallen angels condemned to remain on earth**; nature spirits, or small human beings. **They are said to have magical powers and to consort with witches** and other humans with supernatural powers. . ."
(Geddes and Grosett, *Guide to the Occult and Mysticism,* p. 446)

The popular occult "field guide" titled, ***A Field Guide to Demons, Fairies, Fallen Angels*** and Other Subversive Spirits (by Carol K. Mack and Dinah Mack) readily link demons and fallen angels with fairies.

Fairies also represent the disembodied spirits of Halloween, **and Christians knew them to be "demons"**. *The Woman's Dictionary of Symbols and Sacred Objects* says:

"In Ireland, all the sidh or fairy hills (grave mounds) were said to open up on the occasion [Halloween]. Folks insisted that it was impossible to keep **the fairies**

underground on Halloween. **Since these fairies were simply pagan spirits, the church naturally insisted that demons** were abroad on Halloween." (Walker, Barbara, *The Woman's Dictionary of Symbols and Sacred Objects,* p. 180)

The popular *Encyclopedia of Occultism* by Lewis Spence, **connects fairies to the devil** ands says of fairies, **"They steal human children, and leave in their places fairy changelings. . ."** (Lewis Spence, *Encyclopedia of Occultism,* p. 154)

Dr. Kurt Koch, probably the world's greatest authority on demonism, writes of fairies in *Occult ABC*:

"If a person wants their [fairies] help, **he must apply to their chief, the devil himself**. This however, would cost a person his salvation. **The idea that these spirits [fairies] are demonic is in accordance with the Bible**."
(Dr. Kurt Koch, *Occult ABC,* p. 83)

According to *The Encyclopedia of Witches and Witchcraft*, **"Fairies are fallen angels."** It goes on to describe fairies as, **"Some fairies were said to suck human blood like vampires**. . . Many contemporary Witches believe in fairies and some see them clairvoyantly. **Some Witches say their Craft (WitchCraft) was passed down from fairies . . .**"
(Rosemary Ellen Guiley, *The Encyclopedia of Witches and Witchcraft,* p. 117)

Fairies come from the underground of hell. "Fairies are generally believed to live as a nation in an underground location. . ." *(Harpers' Encyclopedia of Mystical & Paranormal Experience*, p. 198)

Witchcraft in the Church

Another enlightening artistic addition on the *Payable on Death* album is P.O.D.'s "personal occult symbols". Personal "symbols" are a common practice in the occult. *Harpers' Encyclopedia of Mystical & Paranormal Experience* states, "**Symbols are important to all esoteric teachings**, for they contain secret wisdom accessible only to the initiated." (*Harpers' Encyclopedia of Mystical & Paranormal Experience*, p.594)

ZEPPELIN's PERSONAL SYMBOLS

Like P.O.D., the occult soaked rock group Led Zeppelin also introduced personal occult symbols on one of their albums. Guitarist Jimmy Page of Zeppelin is a devout follower of Satanist and self-proclaimed "The Beast 666", Aleister Crowley. In 1971, guitarist Jimmy Page bought Crowley's Boleskine House on the shore of Loch Ness where Crowley practiced his hellish, satanic sex-magick rituals, including human sacrifices. Guitarist Jimmy Page actually performed Crowley magical rituals during their concerts. Their song "Stairway to Heaven" carries the reference "May Queen", which is the name of a hideous poem by Crowley. Page had inscribed in the vinyl of their album Led Zeppelin III, Crowley's famous "Do what thou wilt. So mete it Be'. Page and Robert Plant claim some of Zeppelins' songs came via occultic "automatic handwriting", including their popular "Stairway to Heaven". Stephen Davis in the Hammer of the Gods, details the occult inspiration of "Stairway to Heaven".

Hélèné Fulton

". . . Robert described the 'automatic' nature of the lyric: 'I was just sitting there with Pagey in front of a fire at Headley Grange. Pagey had written the chords and played them for me. I was holding a paper and pencil, and for some reason, I was in a very bad mood. **Then all of a sudden my hand was writing out words. 'There's a lady who's sure, all that glitters is gold, and she's buying a stairway to heaven.' I just sat there and looked at the words and then I almost leaped out of my seat.'"** (Stephen Davis, *Hammer of the Gods*, p. 164)

"He [Robert Palmer] often remarked that he could feel his pen being pushed by some higher authority." (Stephen Davis, *Hammer of the Gods*, p. 262)

There is no doubt to the occult influence of Led Zeppelin. For a very through, extensively documented history of Zeppelin's occult inspiration read the 648 page book titled, *Fallen Angel: The Untold Story of Jimmy Page and Led Zeppelin* by Thomas Friend.

Zeppelin's "personal symbols" were etched in occult images. For instance, "Zoso" was Jimmy Page's personal symbol and according to Stephen Davis in *The Hammer of the Gods* (p. 253), it is a "stylized 666". To further document Page's "Zoso" emblem's connection to satanist Crowley and the number 666, the following page is from Crowley's book *The Equinox of the Gods*(p. 253):

> So is O.
> O = A in the Book of Thoth (The Tarot).
> A = 111 with all its great meanings, ☉ = 6.
> Now 666 = My name.
>   = the number of the stélé.
>   = the number of the Beast. (See Apocalypse.)
>   = the number of the ☉

Witchcraft in the Church

Like Zeppelin, P.O.D.'s "personal symbols" **(BELOW)** are also etched in occult imagery. I asked Dr. Cathy Burns, author of several exhaustive books on occult symbols and a recognized authority on symbology, to evaluate P.O.D.'s "personal occult symbols". Along with several pages of detailed documentation linking P.O.D.'s symbols to the occult, Dr. Burns stated their symbols, ". . . **look wicked and occulitc"**. (personal letter on file)

P.O.D.'s PERSONAL SYMBOLS

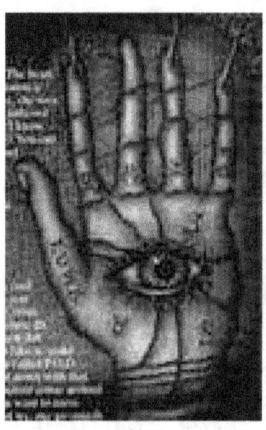

On P.O.D.'s CD liner is also the familiar "eye in the palm" **(ABOVE)**. This is a widely known occult symbol of divination and palmistry. Many fortune-tellers and palm readers display the "eye in the palm" advertising their occult practice. Dr. Cathy Burns writes of the eye in the palm**,** "When the eyes are situated in the hand, for example, **by association with the symbolism of the hand they come to denote clairvoyant action (divination).**"

(Dr. Cathy Burns, *Masonic and Occult Symbols Illustrated*, p. 384)

The Woman's Dictionary of Symbols & Sacred Objects, "**The entire field of palmistry is summed up in this symbol** [eye in the palm] implying that insight is to be found in the palm of the hand." (Barbara G. Walker, *The Woman's Dictionary of Symbols & Sacred Objects*, p 321)

P.O.D.'s "eye in the hand" also contains several occult astrology symbols, the Latin word "LUNA" for "MOON" and P.O.D.'s personal symbols.

It is also VERY revealing that the P.O.D. "eye in the hand" is the "left" hand. In case you do not know, Satanism is commonly known as the "left hand path". *The Dictionary of Cults, Sects, Religions and the Occult* writers, **"Left Hand path (occult). Term used in the occult circles synonymous with evil.** In the Bible, the goats (wicked) got to the left hand of God to be separated for judgement, while the sheep (righteous) go to the right to be saved." (Mather, George A. and Larry Nichols, *The Dictionary of Cults, Sects, Religions and the Occult*, p. 175)

Also, on the hand is the letter "S" Hmmm. . . I wonder whose name begins with the letter "S"? Who is commonly known by the letter "S"? I'll give a hint. He tempted Jesus in Matthew 4. (as in Satan) In astrology the letter "S" is also used for Saturn. According to researcher Dr. Cathy Burns, **"Saturn is really Satan"**. (Dr. Cathy Burns, *Masonic and Occult Symbols Illustrated*, p. 314)

There is the bizarre occurrence of the "cursed" number 13. The number 13 is a major player in the occult, death and Satanism. Throughout the Bible the number thirteen is plainly connected to Satan and rebellion. Ed Vallowe writes in

Witchcraft in the Church

Biblical Mathematics, **"The number thirteen is associated with depravity and rebellion. This number is usually associated with evil. . ."** (Ed Vallowe, *Biblical Mathematics,* p. 102) Author N.W. Hutchings says of the number thirteen, "Thirteen is one of the most interesting of all numbers. **It is clearly associated with rebellion**." (N.W. Hutchings, *God, The Master Mathematican,* p. 29)

Satan himself, is represented by the number 13. The prestigious *Dictionary of Symbolism* documents the devil as the number 13, "The devil was believed to accompany a coven of 12 witches **as the 13th member**" (Hans Biedermann, *Dictionary of Symbolism*, p. 241)

According to the Jewish Cabalist, **the number 13 represents the Snake, the dragon, Satan.** <Symbolism and Properties, pages.globetrotter.net/sdesr/nuprop.htm>

The book, *Satan Wants You, The Cult of Devil Worship in America*, links the number thirteen with Satan and says, "**It is symbolic of death or the unknown**." (Arthur Lyons, *Satan Wants You, The Cult of Devil Worship in America,* p. 38)

The number thirteen in the satanic Tarot card is "DEATH". (ON RIGHT) Notice the number "13" on the BOTTOM LEFT and the Roman Numeral for Thirteen "XIII" at the TOP.

Hélèné Fulton
It's not surprising the thirteenth chapter of the Revelation describes the Antichrist.

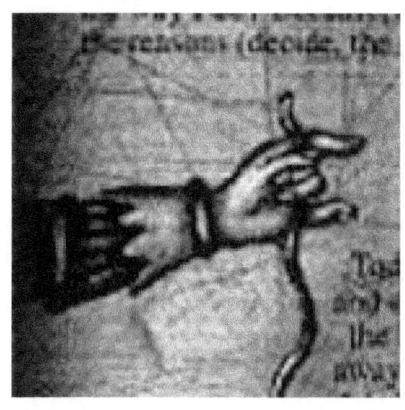

The most frightening symbol on the P.O.D. CD liner is a subtle (see Genesis 3:1) display of the popular hand gesture known as the "Horned Hand" or the Satanic Salute **(ON LEFT)**. Technically known as the "Cornuto", (cornuto is Latin for "horn") it is a well-established symbol of Satanism. **Note: This is NOT the "I love you" sign language where the thumb is extended**. The book, *Satanism in America* writes, **"The 'Horned Hand' is the sign of recognition between those who are in the occult. . ."** (Fletcher Brothers, *Satanism in America*, p.42)

The "satanic salute" goes back many years and according to *The Woman's Dictionary of Symbols & Sacred Objects*, is an **"appeal to the devil"** - "In antiquity it must have represented an appeal to **the Horned God**; then in the Middle Ages, **an appeal to the devil. . ."** (*The Woman's Dictionary of Symbols & Sacred Objects*, p. 308)

Satanist Anton LaVey is shown forming the "Cornuto" on the back of *The Satanic Bible*. The "Horned Hand" is also flashed during the Satanic Black Mass. It is no accident, nor coincidence; it appears on P.O.D.'s CD liner. A careful look at the "salute" in P.O.D.'s album clearly reveals the deliberate intention of forming the "satanic salute". **Nobody naturally holds a rope (or root) with their hand in the "Satanic salute" position**. It is also worth mentioning, the hand is again the "left hand".

Witchcraft in the Church

The Satanic Salute

The back of The Satanic Bible. Anton LaVey's bottom hand is making the "salute".

A Satanic Black Mass.
Notice the people making the Satanic Salute.

Hélèné Fulton

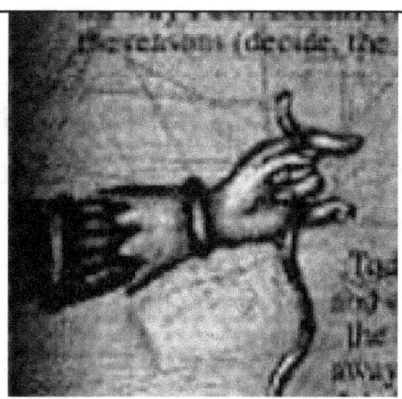

The Satanic Salute from P.O.D.'s album.

The "I Love You" Sign Language. Notice, the thumb is extended.

**There is so much occult imagery on P.O.D.'s CD I could go on and on and on. . . .
For instance, there is the constant "death" theme.**

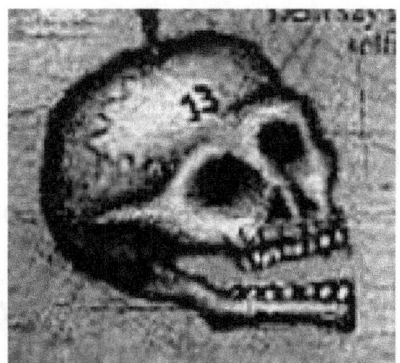

Throughout the P.O.D. album is an unhealthy preoccupation with "death". In the CD liner is a skull wearing on the forehead, the "death number" of 13 **(ON LEFT)**. Dr. Burns writes of the skull, **"It is prominent in witchcraft and demon worship as a celebration of death."** (Dr. Cathy Burns, *Masonic and Occult Symbols Illustrated*, p. 388)

Even P.O.D.'s name stands for Payable on **Death**. P.O.D. claims the name signifies that at "death" a Christian "cashes in" hence, the "payable on death". But this is a serious doctrinal error and again indicates a confused spiritual condition.

The Bible clearly teaches the "devil" is the author and promoter of death. And the Lord Jesus Christ is the author and promoter of life.

Hebrews 2:14 says the "devil (not the Lord Jesus) is the power of "death".

[14] Forasmuch then as the children are partakers of flesh and blood, he also himself likewise took part of the same; that through death he might destroy him that **had the power of death, that is, the devil;**

Hebrews 2:14 (KJV)

In Revelation 6, the entrance of the antichrist is foretold. And his name was "death" – and "hell" followed him.

[8] And I looked, and behold a pale horse: and his name that sat on him was Death, and Hell followed with him. And power was given unto them over the fourth part of the earth, to kill with sword, and with hunger, and with death, and with the beasts of the earth.

Revelation 6:8 (KJV)

As Satan glorifies and testifies of "death". **So does P.O.D.** As we have clearly seen, their *Payable on Death* album is covered with occult images of DEATH. They claim their name Payable on Death represents when a Christian "dies" then their salvation is "paid", hence "Payable on Death". **Nothing could be further from the truth!** A Christian's "salvation" was paid completely and totally by the Lord Jesus Christ at Calvary! And the second a sinner trusts in the shed blood of the Lord Jesus their salvation is completely paid. Not at death!

The fascination P.O.D. has with "death" is a very, very serious spiritual problem.

Just as Satan and P.O.D. glorifies and testifies of "death", the Lord Jesus glorifies and testifies of LIFE! Hundreds of verses could be given to show the Lord Jesus is the author of life.

⁴ In him was life; and the life was the light of men.

John 1:4 (KJV)

⁴⁰ And ye will not come to me, that ye might have life.

John 5:40 (KJV)

³⁵ And Jesus said unto them, I am the bread of life: he that cometh to me shall never hunger; and he that believeth on me shall never thirst.

⁴⁸ I am that bread of life.

John 6:35, 48 (KJV)

²⁵ Jesus said unto her, I am the resurrection, and the life: he that believeth in me, though he were dead, yet shall he live:

Witchcraft in the Church

²⁶ And whosoever liveth and believeth in me shall never die. Believest thou this?

John 11:25-26 (KJV)

⁶ Jesus saith unto him, I am the way, the truth, and the life: no man cometh unto the Father, but by me.

John 14:6 (KJV)

Daniel Martin Diaz
The artwork for Payable on death was created by artist Daniel Martin Diaz.
One reviewer describes Diaz's art as:
"A common iconography runs through all the drawings: **Diaz's world is made up of scorpions and snakes, skulls and detached limbs, crucifixions and saints, astrological symbols and hearts on fire**."
(Joshua Rose, *Shade Magazine*, "Thirty-One Drawings in Thirty-One Days", June & July, 2004)
One of Diaz's esoteric drawings is titled *Magicus,* which depicts the head of a woman on the body of a moth, with four eyes covering the wings. Though the head is crowned, the body ends with the tail of a scorpion. **Under the figure, Diaz has written in script the words to Hail Mary in Latin**.
The demonic number thirteen also appears in much of Diaz's works.
LA Times describes Diaz's, sick and perverted drawing titled *Life*: "In one drawing, called 'Life,' we find a crowned Virgin Mary connected through an umbilical cord that stems from a cross around her neck to **a free-floating, half-reptilian fetus (characterized elsewhere as Jesus)." Can you believe such blasphemy?** The

Hélèné Fulton

Lord Jesus as satanic "half-reptilian"? May I remind you – Satan is the serpent or reptile of Genesis 3 – not the Lord Jesus!!! The picture also has written "13 Christi Fetus".

LA Times describes another Diaz demonic disaster called *Crown of Thorns* (an obvious reference to the Lord Jesus) as, "'Crown of Thorns' portrays an emaciated torso that gives way to tree roots below the waist, **two severed arms**, extended as if on a cross, **and a single thorn-encircled eye where the head would be**." God helps us! **What sick, perverted, wicked, and ungodly blasphemy. And P.O.D. plasters Diaz's spiritual perversion on their album cover!** For a view of some of Diaz's sick art http://wiredheart.hispeed.com/july03/daniel_martin_diaz.html This site is a picture of Jesus on the cross as a scorpion with the number 13.http://www.jqadams.com/gallery/diaz.html

You Christian young people that continue to defend P.O.D. you better wake up! If you keep on defending and making excuses for people that blaspheme and pervert the Lord Jesus Christ, you will pay serious spiritual consequences. You cannot fill your heart and your mind with the music of P.O.D. and remain spiritually sound. It has already spiritually corrupted many of you reading this article. You already place P.O.D. way above the Lord Jesus. You're mad at me for the documented TRUTH in this article. And yet you tolerate, defend and "love" this music from people that mock and pervert your Saviour! God help you. . . Wake Up! (Romans 13:11)

Daniel Martin Diaz website (P.O.D.'s artist) has an open invitation and initiation into occult divination. Diaz proudly broadcasts the following on his website: "Divination: the art or practice that seeks to foresee or foretell future events or discover hidden knowledge. by the interpretation of omens or by the aid of supernatural powers." **Diaz has even included on his website downloadable occult objects and images to practice satanic divination!** Diaz's website says, **"These symbols can be used in meditation or as a divinatory tool to unlock the power of the subconscious"** The pages contain occult symbols in the shape of a cube or a cross. **You download the images, cut along the dotted lines and construct your own occult image to induce demon possession!** One of the pages is titled, "cubus", in which you cut out and create an "occult dice". Diaz's instructions says, **"Roll dice, meditate on symbol. Discover hidden mysteries within yourself**. Try rolling more than one. Create your own meaning for each symbol".

The Lord is very, very clear about the satanic practice of DIVINATION.

[9] When thou art come into the land which the LORD thy God giveth thee, thou shalt not learn to do after the abominations of those nations.

[10] There shall not be found among you any one that maketh his son or his daughter to pass through the fire, or that useth divination, or an observer of times, or an enchanter, or a witch.

[11] Or a charmer, or a consulter with familiar spirits, or a wizard, or a necromancer.

Hélèné Fulton

¹² For all that do these things are an abomination unto the LORD: and because of these abominations the LORD thy God doth drive them out from before thee.

Deuteronomy 18:9-12 (KJV)

17 In the twelfth year of Ahaz king of Judah began Hoshea the son of Elah to reign in Samaria over Israel nine years.

² And he did that which was evil in the sight of the LORD, but not as the kings of Israel that were before him.

³ Against him came up Shalmaneser king of Assyria; and Hoshea became his servant, and gave him presents.

⁴ And the king of Assyria found conspiracy in Hoshea: for he had sent messengers to So king of Egypt, and brought no present to the king of Assyria, as he had done year by year: therefore the king of Assyria shut him up, and bound him in prison.

⁵ Then the king of Assyria came up throughout all the land, and went up to Samaria, and besieged it three years.

⁶ In the ninth year of Hoshea the king of Assyria took Samaria, and carried Israel away into Assyria, and placed them in Halah and in Habor by the river of Gozan, and in the cities of the Medes.

⁷ For so it was, that the children of Israel had sinned against the LORD their God, which had brought them up out of the land of Egypt, from under the hand of Pharaoh king of Egypt, and had feared other gods,

⁸ And walked in the statutes of the heathen, whom the LORD cast out from before the children of Israel, and of the kings of Israel, which they had made.

⁹ And the children of Israel did secretly those things that were not right against the LORD their God, and they built them high places in all their cities, from the tower of the watchmen to the fenced city.

¹⁰ And they set them up images and groves in every high hill, and under every green tree:

¹¹ And there they burnt incense in all the high places, as did the heathen whom the LORD carried away before them; and wrought wicked things to provoke the LORD to anger:

Witchcraft in the Church

¹² For they served idols, whereof the LORD had said unto them, Ye shall not do this thing.

¹³ Yet the LORD testified against Israel, and against Judah, by all the prophets, and by all the seers, saying, Turn ye from your evil ways, and keep my commandments and my statutes, according to all the law which I commanded your fathers, and which I sent to you by my servants the prophets.

¹⁴ Notwithstanding they would not hear, but hardened their necks, like to the neck of their fathers, that did not believe in the LORD their God.

¹⁵ And they rejected his statutes, and his covenant that he made with their fathers, and his testimonies which he testified against them; and they followed vanity, and became vain, and went after the heathen that were round about them, concerning whom the LORD had charged them, that they should not do like them.

¹⁶ And they left all the commandments of the LORD their God, and made them molten images, even two calves, and made a grove, and worshipped all the host of heaven, and served Baal.

¹⁷ And they caused their sons and their daughters to pass through the fire, **and used divination and enchantments, and sold themselves to do evil in the sight of the LORD, to provoke him to anger**.

¹⁸ Therefore the LORD was very angry with Israel, and removed them out of his sight: there was none left but the tribe of Judah only.

¹⁹ Also Judah kept not the commandments of the LORD their God, but walked in the statutes of Israel which they made.

²⁰ And the LORD rejected all the seed of Israel, and afflicted them, and delivered them into the hand of spoilers, until he had cast them out of his sight.

²¹ For he rent Israel from the house of David; and they made Jeroboam the son of Nebat king: and Jeroboam drave Israel from following the LORD, and made them sin a great sin.

²² For the children of Israel walked in all the sins of Jeroboam which he did; they departed not from them;

²³ Until the LORD removed Israel out of his sight, as he had said by all his servants the prophets. So was Israel carried away out of their own land to Assyria unto this day.

²⁴ And the king of Assyria brought men from Babylon, and from Cuthah, and from Ava, and from Hamath, and from Sepharvaim, and placed them in the cities of Samaria instead of the children of Israel: and they possessed Samaria, and dwelt in the cities thereof.

²⁵ And so it was at the beginning of their dwelling there, that they feared not the LORD: therefore the LORD sent lions among them, which slew some of them.

²⁶ Wherefore they spake to the king of Assyria, saying, The nations which thou hast removed, and placed in the cities of Samaria, know not the manner of the God of the land: therefore he hath sent lions among them, and, behold, they slay them, because they know not the manner of the God of the land.

²⁷ Then the king of Assyria commanded, saying, Carry thither one of the priests whom ye brought from thence; and let them go and dwell there, and let him teach them the manner of the God of the land.

²⁸ Then one of the priests whom they had carried away from Samaria came and dwelt in Bethel, and taught them how they should fear the LORD.

²⁹ Howbeit every nation made gods of their own, and put them in the houses of the high places which the Samaritans had made, every nation in their cities wherein they dwelt.

³⁰ And the men of Babylon made Succothbenoth, and the men of Cuth made Nergal, and the men of Hamath made Ashima,

³¹ And the Avites made Nibhaz and Tartak, and the Sepharvites burnt their children in fire to Adrammelech and Anammelech, the gods of Sepharvaim.

³² So they feared the LORD, and made unto themselves of the lowest of them priests of the high places, which sacrificed for them in the houses of the high places.

³³ They feared the LORD, and served their own gods, after the manner of the nations whom they carried away from thence.

³⁴ Unto this day they do after the former manners: they fear not the LORD, neither do they after their statutes, or after their ordinances, or

Witchcraft in the Church

after the law and commandment which the LORD commanded the children of Jacob, whom he named Israel;

³⁵ With whom the LORD had made a covenant, and charged them, saying, Ye shall not fear other gods, nor bow yourselves to them, nor serve them, nor sacrifice to them:

³⁶ But the LORD, who brought you up out of the land of Egypt with great power and a stretched out arm, him shall ye fear, and him shall ye worship, and to him shall ye do sacrifice.

³⁷ And the statutes, and the ordinances, and the law, and the commandment, which he wrote for you, ye shall observe to do for evermore; and ye shall not fear other gods.

³⁸ And the covenant that I have made with you ye shall not forget; neither shall ye fear other gods.

³⁹ But the LORD your God ye shall fear; and he shall deliver you out of the hand of all your enemies.

⁴⁰ Howbeit they did not hearken, but they did after their former manner.

⁴¹ So these nations feared the LORD, and served their graven images, both their children, and their children's children: as did their fathers, so do they unto this day.

2 King 17 (KJV)

By the way, P.O.D.'s website has a link to Diaz's occult and divination website. **And on the special Playstation Game, P.O.D. has a special feature segment on Diaz! WOW!**

Diaz's website contain "hidden"(meta keywords) search words and phrases. **These are words that Diaz uses to best describe his site.** The web visitor does not see these "search" words, but search engines such as google, yahoo, etc. can "see" them. Search words are words that best describe the web site. If you type in any of these "hidden" search words, Google will "see" them and return Diaz's site as a valid hit. What are some of

Hélèné Fulton

Diaz's "hidden" and descriptive search words? **"dark art, mystic Christ. Shamanic, Shamanic art**, Astrology. . . **shamanism. . . Alchemical Healing**, metaphysics, personal transformation. **Shamanic Journey, shamanic energy healing, ceremonial ritual, esoteric, magickal, devil, satan, 666, Demonic Attack**,The Rite of Exorcism, **Devil or demon on** oath. . . **My name is Legion**, horkizo, Mark 5:1-13. . .chakra. . . **dementia, guts, gore**, music, hell, **serialkillers, crime, blood, dark,occult, paranormal, witchcraft**, dead bodies, halloween, corpses, gruesome, **Dark and demented portal site geared to unusual aspects of life"**

Diaz is also a member of the gothic band **Blind Divine**. The following occult and witchcraft websites (among many others) that link to Diaz's website and art.

- Wicca (Witchcraft) Chat Room @ www.wicca-chat.com/links/artwork.htm
- Darkness Rising @ www.darknessrising.com
- Deviant Art @ beauty-fiend.deviantart.com
- Death and Dementia @ www.deathndementia.com
- Galactica Publishing -"The journal of Paganism, Occultism, Mysticism, Existentialism and Western Culture" @ www.galacticapublishing.com/links.php
- Anathema Occult Books @ www.anathemabooks.com/art.shtml
- Dark Side of the Net @ www.darklinks.com
- Dark sites @ www.darksites.com

My young Christian friend, I know you do not fully understand the spiritual danger of this stuff. And I know music can grab you and influence you – **but leave this stuff alone!** You cannot possibly imagine the spiritual danger you are embracing. This is not just music. **You are opening your**

heart and soul to something serious and sinister. STAY AWAY!

Pagan gods

In January 2012 I was out shopping with a friend helping her to find things to put in her new Guest House. We were in a shopping mall in Durban called Game City. We were standing about 3 meters from an entrance where they sell Indian clothing like Sari's and in the doorway of this shop was a huge golden Elephant (Genesha) one of the many Hindu gods.

This one the son of Shiva (The most powerful and fascinating deity in Hinduism, who represents death and dissolution. One of the godheads in the Hindu Trinity, and known by many names - Mahadeva, Pashupati, Nataraja, Vishwanath, BholeNath - Shiva is perhaps the most complex of Hindu deities. Hindus recognise this by putting his shrine in the temple separate from those of other deities and worshipping Shiva as a phallic symbol called the 'Shiva Limgam' in most temples.) Parvati, Ganesha is depicted as having a curved trunk and big ears, and a huge pot-bellied body of a human being. He is the lord of success and destroyer of evils and obstacles. He is also worshipped as the god of knowledge, wisdom and wealth.

So as we were standing there I said: "How can anyone pray to such an ugly thing" Not very long after this we were walking to a coffee shop to get some lunch and I suddenly felt a very cold stroke over my head, It felt like someone was stroking my hair like that which mothers or fathers would do. I immediately rebuked it as this is what The Holy Spirit advised me to do. As we were sitting down at a Coffee shop having lunch I could feel the Fire of the Holy Spirit on my head on the area where the stroke was.

Because I said Ganesha is ugly, the demon associated with him tried to steal my knowledge, wisdom and wealth (prosperity), but because I'm protected by the Fire of the Holy Spirit he could not do this.

Now to anyone not knowing that this was not a normal wind just blowing on your hair this could have been very dangerous. You need to have the guidance of The Holy Spirit and you need to be protected especially because you are Prayer Eagles and you will play a very significant and important role in the ministry regardless of where you are situated. Remember you are kings and queens in the Kingdom of the King of kings.

They have tried after this again a few months later. This time it felt like something is pulling something from my head. It is soft and you get almost a type of Goosebumps on the spot. Be aware to rebuke it. A demon is trying to steal your knowledge. You might even find that after this happened you battle to concentrate or remember things. You will also battle to read your Bible and pray. See the prayer at the end of this chapter.

Please note never ever attack a pagan god if you were not told so by God himself. Please read the true story below.

3 Pastors went from Johannesburg to Durban (Chatsworth) with the mission to rebuke the demons in one of the biggest temples (pagan god) in Chatsworth. This was not the will of God and they were not commanded by God to do so. The

Witchcraft in the Church

senior pastor started rebuking the demons associated with this religion from across the road. The demons fired their fiery darts and of course this pastor was not baptized by the Fire of the Holy Spirit and this pastor lost his breastplate of righteousness due to the fact he was doing this out of their own will and not in obedience to God, he was severely injured. He was taken to the local emergency clinic but although he was dying, doctors could not find anything wrong with him. They told the other two pastors to take him home. None of the doctors were born again and the other two pastors did not even have discernment. They took him home and he passed away the next day. If they only started praying for the pastor but they did not even do that.

If you suddenly get a sharp pain without an injury, be aware someone is sending voodoo to you. Immediately say out loud: (pointing to the spot) This pain is not mine I send it back to the sender (Satan) 100 fold in the name of Jesus Christ.

This is not witchcraft if you send it back. You are merely returning a gift that you do not want and did not ask for.

Always wash the food and liquids that you are about to consume with the blood of Jesus Christ before you eat or drink it.

I am under constant attack. Why? Because of my work. Satan does not like it one bit that people are being informed. He also does not like people being saved. If you are a born again believer you will be under attack. But do not fear as God has given us the full armor as per Ephesians 6. We also have the Blood of Jesus Christ and the Fire of the Holy Spirit.

[12] For we do not wrestle against flesh and blood, but against principalities, against powers, against the rulers of the darkness of this age, against spiritual *hosts* of wickedness in the heavenly *places.*
[13] Therefore take up the whole armor of God, that you may be able to withstand in the evil day, and having done all, to stand.
[14] Stand therefore, having girded your waist with truth, having put on the breastplate of righteousness, [15] and having shod your feet with the preparation of the gospel of peace; [16] above all, taking the shield of faith with which you will be able to quench all the fiery darts of the wicked one. [17] And take the helmet of salvation, and the sword of the Spirit, which is the word of God; [18] praying always with all prayer and supplication in the Spirit, being watchful to this end with all perseverance and supplication for all the saints— [19] and for me, that utterance may be given to me, that I may open my mouth boldly to make known the mystery of the gospel, [20] for which I am an ambassador in chains; that in it I may speak boldly, as I ought to speak.

Ephesians 6:12-20

Never take any illness as God created us without sickness!

Any object that was used in any form of the occult or in any pagan religion is cursed and you as a Christian should not touch, wear or keep it.

Prayer
In the name of Jesus Christ, I bind Satan and all his demons. You have no authority over me as I belong to Father God and Satan you have been defeated 2000 years ago by Jesus Christ on the cross.

Witchcraft in the Church

In the name of Jesus Christ, I reclaim and loose all the things that Satan has stolen from me, (say your name and surname here).

In the name of Jesus Christ, upon my, (say your name and surname here) mind I, (say your name and surname here) take back all my knowledge, spiritual knowledge, revelation, insight, understanding, wisdom, truth, discernment, diligent searching, freedom and through Jesus Christ I ask that this will be sealed with the Blood of Jesus Christ never to be taken again.

I ask this in the name of Jesus Christ. Amen.

Chapter 12: The Truth about Spirit Guides

[15]When a psychic told me twenty odd years ago my son's life was in danger and my spirit guides were trying to warn me, I was both alarmed and confused. Prior to this, I'd never heard of spirit guides. The only spirits I believed in at that point were the ones that were haunting my house.

The psychic said my spirit guides were too strong for her, and that they were giving her a terrible headache. She said I would have to find a way for them to speak directly to me. "Just be sure to light a candle and surround yourself with a protective white light before speaking to a spirit," she said. "Make the spirit say it's of the light. A *dark* spirit can't claim to be of the light. God won't allow it."

I went home that day and fashioned a makeshift pendulum, then drew an alphabet arc on a sheet of paper. Heart in my throat, I spoke to the air: "If there's a spirit of light here that wants to talk to me about my son, if you'll swing the pendulum over the letters, we'll be able to communicate."

---

[15] True life experience by Stacie Spielman

Witchcraft in the Church

Immediately the pendulum began to swing, and I wasn't the one swinging it: "My name is Gideon. I'm of the light. I am your Guardian Angel."

As it turned out, the danger my son had been in was already past. The dangerous incident had already happened and my son was unharmed. But having contacted my "Guardian Angel" and actually carried on a conversation with him via the pendulum, I was hooked. This was the beginning of my seven-year sojourn with my "Guardian Angel" and other "spirits of light" he introduced me to.

My favourite of the spirit guides Gideon introduced me to Saul. Saul was to become my healing guide. He trained me to pull pain out of people's bodies in the form of negative energy, and taught me to do "psychic diagnoses" by closing my eyes and moving my hands close to the person's body without touching. When my hands passed over an area of good health, I would see various shades of green through my mind's eye, depending on how healthy the tissue was. In areas of pain, I would see varying shades of red, depending on the severity of the pain. In areas of dying tissue, I would see grey. For dead tissue, I'd see black. I only experienced black one time, and that was with a man who had just died.

At first my only method of talking to my guides was through the pendulum and alphabet arc. But my guides soon grew tired of this and began speaking telepathically. In the presence of my guides I felt more love than I've ever felt from a human.

Hélèné Fulton

Telepathic communication is typical of spirit guides. Some, however, prefer to communicate through dreams, through a hypnotic state, or through automatic writing. In the case of Sylvia Browne, for example, when her spirit guide Francine speaks through her, Sylvia must make a recording and listen to it at a later time.

My former guides represented themselves as angelic entities that was once been human. In the case of Shamanism, the spirit guides represent themselves as animals. In New Age, the guides claim to be ascended masters (including Buddha and Jesus himself). For still others, guides choose to represent themselves as the spirit of a dead loved one.

Archetypal Guides are those who supposedly come into a person's life to guide him/her through a difficult problem. They typically represent themselves as a warrior, a story teller, a wise old man, etc.

During the course of my former ministry, I worked with many harassment victims who'd had spirit guides. Some of these spirit guides had claimed to be angels, some to be a grandmother or distant ancestor, some to be God or Jesus, and some had represented themselves as a tiger, a wolf, or other animal totem. In every case, without exception - even when the guide had claimed to be God or Jesus - when the guides were addressed during cast away, they manifested (did something to the harassment victim to make their presence known) as demons.

Gross though it may be, it was during the time frame of my former ministry that I went for a colonic. I had no idea till we were in the midst of it that the woman doing the colonic was into New Age, or that she conducted weekly seminars to teach her clients how to contact their spirit guides.

When she invited me to attend her class, I of course told her my story and ended by saying that all spirit guides are demonic. At that point, her guide began speaking to her telepathically. "Poor Stacie," it said. "She got involved with bad guides. *Yours* are good ones."

This is so typical it's laughable. Any time someone has a bad experience with the spirit realm, guides all over the world will tell their "wards" that those were bad spirits. The ones working with *them* are good.

When I had my former staciespielman.com website, a woman sent me a drawing her spirit guide had drawn (through taking control of her hand) of itself. When she saw the cover of my book Betrayed by Her Guardian Angel, she was shocked to see that the crude picture her spirit guide had drawn appeared to be an attempted replica of the painting of *my* false Guardian Angel as it appeared on the cover of my book. That picture is shown below.

This spirit guide told the woman "Stacie's website is right when she warns against getting involved with spirit guides. But you don't have to worry, because I'm of the light."

After this woman read my book, she confronted her spirit guide. When she pointed out that my guides had turned out to be demonic, her guide revealed its true identity as well. It, like Gideon and Saul, was a demon.

[16]*I remember a deliverance which I did via Skype. The lady (22 years) was born into Satanism and wanted out.*

Every time I mentioned Jesus's name she would scream and shout and tell me to stop. I asked her why. She told me that Satan had a demon called Jesus that torments them when they are doing something wrong.

I had to bind all the demons around her and then I explained to her what the real Jesus Christ of Nazareth did for her on the cross.

It was only after this that I truly understood why God wanted me to add "God loves you" to the top of our ministries website (www.lighttheworldministries.co.za) and not Jesus loves you like I wanted to.

---

[16] Hélèné Fulton

Chapter 13: Tattoos and Body Piercing

I know this topic will be a very sensitive one for many people. As you all know, many people like to get different types of tattoos and body piercing put on the different parts of their bodies.

You will see people getting tattoos on just about any part of the human anatomy, even on their most intimate, personal, and private parts. The same goes with the different types of body piercing. You have people getting piercing on their noses, navels, eyelids, nipples, tongues, and genitalia.

For those of you who really want to know what the Lord may think about this issue, I would challenge each and every one of you to go before God in prayer and ask for His direct opinion on this matter. I know there is lot of differences in opinion in the Body of Christ on this issue.

On the one side are those who believe that God's command back to the Jewish people in the Book of Leviticus no longer applies to any of us in this day and age since we are now operating under a New Covenant with Jesus and we are now no longer under the law, but under grace. On the other side are those who believe that this command still applies to everyone in this day and age, and that God has not changed His mind on this issue.

I am going to give you my opinion on this subject through what I have learnt helping others to be freed from bondage. In addition to the verse from Leviticus, I believe there are several other verses that you have to match up with that one to get what God's opinion may really be on this issue.

This is just my own personal interpretation of what I feel God may be trying to tell us in these specific verses. You are each responsible for getting your own answers from the Lord on this issue.

For the record, I do not believe the Lord wants any of His people getting any kinds of tattoos or body piercing put on any parts of their body.

> [28] You shall not make any cuttings in your flesh for the dead, nor tattoo any marks on you: I *am* the LORD.
>
> **Leviticus 19:28**

> [17] "Do not think that I came to destroy the Law or the Prophets. I did not come to destroy but to fulfill. [18] For assuredly, I say to you, till heaven and earth pass away, one jot or one tittle will by no means pass from the law till all is fulfilled.
>
> **Matthew 5:17-18**

> [16] Do you not know that you are the temple of God and *that* the Spirit of God dwells in you?
>
> **1 Corinthians 3:16**

> [19] Or do you not know that your body is the temple of the Holy Spirit *who is* in you, whom you have from God, and you are not your own?
>
> **1 Corinthians 6:19**

> [17] If anyone defiles the temple of God, God will destroy him. For the temple of God is holy, which *temple* you are.
>
> **1 Corinthians 3:17**

Witchcraft in the Church

Reading these verses I think it is very clear what God's opinion on this matter is.

The Bible says that God does not change, that He is the same today as He was yesterday. If God the Father is telling us that homosexuality and anything to do with the occult are abominations in His sight back in the Old Testament, then He is not going to be changing His mind just because we are in New Testament times.

Jesus has stated in these verse, all of the moral laws from His Father have not been done away with at this time, and they will not all be done away with until we get our New Heaven and New Earth. And until that even happens, I believe God wants all of us to do our best to abide by them.

The last three verses listed are all telling us that our bodies have now become the temple of God's Holy Spirit. Notice that God is specifically telling us that it is our human physical bodies that have now become the temple of His Holy Spirit.

Think of the ramifications of this statement – that since our human physical bodies are now literally carrying the Holy Spirit Himself on the inside of us once we have accepted Jesus Christ as our personal Lord and Saviour, that God is now telling us that our physical bodies have now become the actual "temple" of His Holy Spirit.

Notice in the last verse that God is using the words "defiles the temple of God," and that anyone who attempts to defile His holy temple will be destroyed.

God then ends this statement with talking about our physical bodies being the temple of His Holy Spirit. In other words, God does not want our temples, which are our physical bodies, to be defiled in any way, shape, and form. Is putting any kind of tattoo or body piercing on our physical bodies a form of defilement with the Lord? I believe that it may be.

Consider this fact. The Jewish people did not have the Holy Spirit living on the inside of them back in the Old Testament. Jesus had not yet come to die for all of our sins, so the Holy Spirit was not living on the inside of the Jewish people like He is now doing with all New Testament born again believers. This means that the physical bodies of the Jewish people back in those days were not considered to be actual temples of the Lord since they did not have the Holy Spirit living on the inside of them.

So if God the Father is telling His chosen people that He did not want them tattooing or putting any kinds of cuttings into their flesh – and their bodies were not even considered to be the temple of His Holy Spirit back in those Old Testament times – then how much more seriously should this command be taken by all born again New Testament believers, since all of our bodies are now considered to be the actual temple of the Holy Spirit?

Our bodies have now become the temple of the Lord Himself. We are no longer our own. As a result, we should be doing everything we can to glorify our God – which includes glorifying Him in our bodies as the second last verse above is telling us to do. Marking up our bodies with the different kinds of tattoos and body piercing may not be what the Lord had in mind when He is telling us to glorify Him in both our bodies and our spirits.

Again, you will each have to get your own interpretation as to what all of these verses are trying to tell us.

I believe that our physical bodies are now more sacred, more precious, and more special in the Lord's eyes than the four physical walls of any church may be since God is now calling our bodies His temple.

And just as we would never consider marking up or defacing any parts of an actual Christian Church building – in the same way I do not believe that our Lord wants us defacing or marking up any parts of our physical bodies. This is why I believe God made sure to put this specific command in His Word.

When God is using the words "any" tattoos and "any" kinds of cuttings in the flesh, He is not making any exceptions with this kind of activity.

I personally believe that God is letting all of us know, loud and clear, that He does not want any of us marking up our bodies with these kinds of defilement.

We did a deliverance on a young man who had several tattoos. The one on his leg stood out. This man had a smell hanging around him and when he enters a room this smell was overwhelming.

The young man told us that he first noticed these "things" holding him captive after he had the tattoo done on his leg.

This young man was held captive in the dungeons of hell (hades) and the smell around him was the smell of the dungeons. We saw the angels taking the chains off his legs during the deliverance.

Unfortunately this young man fell back into this trap in the dark kingdom and had to come back for a second and a third time. Each time he was held captive in the dungeons. The third time, close to the end of the deliverance, I saw this man on a theatre table with big lights above him just like in theatre. He fell under the power and when he woke up he said he can taste the taste you have in your mouth after an operation.

This young man nearly died. God saved him. He is now living a good life and he has learnt his lesson. I spoke to his mother during December 2013 and she was telling me what a remarkable young man he has turned into. Praise God for giving him another chance.

I know a woman that was saved from Satanism. She has since God saved her decorated her body with tattoos. I have laid this before God and the answer was clear. God does not approve of that.

Now I know you want to ask me what if I got my tattoos before I became born again. You can anoint them with anointing oil (send me an email for the preparation of this – DO NOT buy anointing oil from anyone as you do not know what that person does when he/she thinks no one sees them) and ask God to seal them from opening a door to the dark kingdom.

Jacob had a tattoo of a heart with a thorn bush through it. I have seen this tattoo move at times. When it moves it looked like the thorn bush where squeezing the heart so that the heart actually looked out of place. This tattoo was on the back of his shoulder. When this heart was squeezed Jacob would get angry for no reason and I was always the one he got angry at.

If you got the tattoos after you became born again. I think you need to have a heart to heart talk with Father God.

[17]Body Piercing - A Return to Paganism

In some of the most unexpected places we are confronted by a revival of the old tribal practices of body scarification, body piercing and body mutilation Nose rings, eyebrow rings, belly rings, tongue studs, multiple earrings, nipple rings, tattoos and other disfigurements are more than an identifiable sub-culture – it is all part of an aggressive fashion statement which is challenging the Christian Church.

[28] You shall not make any cuttings in your flesh for the dead, nor tattoo any marks on you: I *am* the LORD.
Leviticus 19:28

Unfortunately, most Church leaders have remained silent on this practice, even while some youth leaders and Bible College students are giving themselves over to body modification.

---

[17] Written by Dr. Peter Hammond

Hélèné Fulton

⁵ 'They shall not make any bald *place* on their heads, nor shall they shave the edges of their beards nor make any cuttings in their flesh. ⁶ They shall be holy to their God and not profane the name of their God, for they offer the offerings of the LORD made by fire, *and* the bread of their God; therefore they shall be holy.

Leviticus 21:5-6

As Christians, we are called to be holy, set apart and different from the world, consecrated to God. "Everybody's doing it" is hardly an argument to justify Christian involvement. They very fact that pagans practice body piercing should be a compelling enough argument against Christians being conformed to the world.

⁹ But you *are* a chosen generation, a royal priesthood, a holy nation, His own special people, that you may proclaim the praises of Him who called you out of darkness into His marvelous light;
1 Peter 2:9

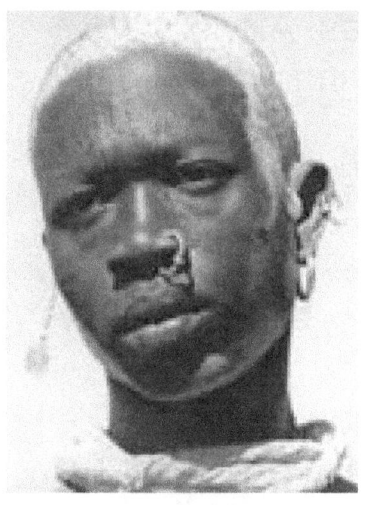

The Scriptures are clear that we must treat our bodies with respect, they are not our own to do with as we wish. They belong to God, who made them and who purchased them with His own blood. Our bodies are to be temples of the Holy Spirit. We are to glorify God with our bodies.

¹⁵ Do you not know that your bodies are members of Christ? Shall I then take the members of Christ and make *them* members of a harlot? Certainly not!

1 Corinthians 6:15, 19-20

Witchcraft in the Church

> ²⁸ So they cried aloud, and cut themselves, as was their custom, with knives and lances, until the blood gushed out on them.
>
> **1 Kings 18:28**

The demon possessed man of Gadara cut himself with stones and ran around naked (Mark 5:5). It was the custom of the Ishmaelite men to wear gold earrings. (Judges 8:24).

Biblically, a pierced ear is a public indication of permanent slavery. When the Hebrews were led out of slavery in Egypt by Moses, they were urged

> *"take off the gold earrings ... so all the people took off their earrings ... These are your gods, O Israel."*
>
> **Exodus 32: 1-3**

After God spoke to Jacob, he instructed his household to get rid of their idols and purify themselves. Along with their stone idols, they buried their earrings.

> ² And Jacob said to his household and to all who *were* with him, "Put away the foreign gods that *are* among you, purify yourselves, and change your garments.
>
> **Genesis 35:2**

This has always been the response of pagan people when they've embraced the Gospel of Christ. From Papau New Guinea to the Amazon jungle, pagan tribes engage in body scarification, earrings, nose rings, tongue studs, multiple piercings and tattoos. Once converted to Christ, however, these tribes abandon all these body modification practices.

¹³ You shall fear the LORD your God and serve Him, and shall take oaths in His name. ¹⁴ You shall not go after other gods, the gods of the peoples who *are* all around you ¹⁵ (for the LORD your God *is* a jealous God among you), lest the anger of the LORD your God be aroused against you and destroy you from the face of the earth.

¹⁶ "You shall not tempt the LORD your God as you tempted *Him* in Massah. ¹⁷ You shall diligently keep the commandments of the LORD your God, His testimonies, and His statutes which He has commanded you.

¹⁸ And you shall do *what is* right and good in the sight of the LORD, that it may be well with you, and that you may go in and possess the good land of which the LORD swore to your fathers, ¹⁹ to cast out all your enemies from before you, as the LORD has spoken.

²⁰ "When your son asks you in time to come, saying, 'What *is the meaning of* the testimonies, the statutes, and the judgments which the LORD our God has commanded you?' ²¹ then you shall say to your son: 'We were slaves of Pharaoh in Egypt, and the LORD brought us out of Egypt with a mighty hand;

Deuteronomy 6:13-21

It is completely inappropriate for a Christian man to wear an earring – the mark of slavery. What may be appropriate for a woman is not necessarily appropriate for a man. What is practiced by the world is seldom acceptable for a Christian.

¹³ For you, brethren, have been called to liberty; only do not *use* liberty as an opportunity for the flesh, but through love serve one another.

Galatians 5:13

¹⁶ as free, yet not using liberty as a cloak for vice, but as bondservants of God.

1 Peter 2:16

5 Stand fast therefore in the liberty by which Christ has made us free, and do not be entangled again with a yoke of bondage.

Galatians 5:1

Witchcraft in the Church

If something is prevalent and accepted in the world, that alone should be a compelling argument against Christians adopting their fashions and fads. We are called to be different. We are to honour God with our bodies.

12 I beseech you therefore, brethren, by the mercies of God, that you present your bodies a living sacrifice, holy, acceptable to God, *which is* your reasonable service. ² And do not be conformed to this world, but be transformed by the renewing of your mind, that you may prove what *is* that good and acceptable and perfect will of God.

Romans 12: 1-2

Our bodies matter. They are to be presented to God as holy offerings – in a way that pleases God. We are not to follow the example of the pagans. Making holes in our bodies is hardly respecting them as temples of the Holy Spirit. Permanently disfiguring our bodies is blatant rebellion to our Creator and Redeemer.

[11] Beloved, I beg *you* as sojourners and pilgrims, abstain from fleshly lusts which war against the soul

1 Peter 2:11

Part of the Biblical description of a harlot is that

I will punish her
For the days of the Baals to which she burned incense.
She decked herself with her earrings and jewelry,
And went after her lovers;
But Me she forgot," says the LORD.

Hosea 2:13

Hélèné Fulton

For he flatters himself in his own eyes,
When he finds out his iniquity *and* when he hates.

Psalm 36:2

Let us search out and examine our ways,
And turn back to the LORD;

Lamentations 3:40

To draw attention to ourselves with these excessive fashion statements is hardly in keeping with the Biblical commands to be humble and modest (Proverbs 21:4; 1 Timothy 2: 9-10)

[3] Do not let your adornment be *merely* outward—arranging the hair, wearing gold, or putting on *fine* apparel— [4] rather *let it be* the hidden person of the heart, with the incorruptible *beauty* of a gentle and quiet spirit, which is very precious in the sight of God.

1 Peter 3: 3-4

The present obsession of many with body modification is a revival of tribalism. It involves a painful initiation rite, which produces an identification with a certain tribe, clan or sub-culture. The Kacipo people in Sudan stretch their lower lips to fit a saucer-sized pottery and they stretch their ear lobes to create huge holes and long earlobes. Amongst the Nuba tribes in Sudan, multiple earrings, nose rings, body scarification and body painting are prevalent. The Dinka and Nuer tribes in Sudan are easily identifiable by the pattern of scars across their foreheads.

Amongst the Hindus - nose studs, belly rings, toe rings, tongue studs and eyebrow rings are common. Tattoos amongst the Amazon tribes identify the various members of a given tribe. In Papau New Guinea, all kinds of body scarification, tattoos and body mutilation distinguish the various tribes.

Witchcraft in the Church

Among the tribes in Borneo, tattooing is mainly associated with head hunting (a visible sign of success) for men and the coming of age of women - in some cases it symbolizes their social status. Tattoos are part of the "rites of passage" and next to blackened teeth and long ear lobes, intricate tattoos on fingers, hands, lower arms, thighs, calves, and feet served as important elements of beauty for women.

A pagan view on the subject: *"A tattoo is a complex signifier: it signals class; it signals sexuality; and it has specific content as a signifier: a depiction of an animal, a person, an abstract tribal design. The most usual motifs are signifiers of power and masculinity... But what the tattoo signals above all is the power one seizes over one's own body… To be branded or tattooed shows also that you have the requisite guts to join the group. It is not the most extreme or painful form of initiation, but it serves as a sign of pain and hence of resolution."* (Crispen Sartwell)

"Tattooing is often a magical rite in the more traditional cultures, and the tattooist is respected as a priest or shaman." (Michelle Delio, Tattoo: The Exotic Art of Skin Decoration, p. 73)

Hélèné Fulton

And in the same way, eyebrow rings, nose rings, multiple earrings, nipple rings, belly rings and tongue studs distinguish identifiable sub-cultures in New York, London, Paris and other capitals of what is meant to be civilization.

"The look on their faces testifies against them; they parade their sin like Sodom; they do not hide it. Woe to them! They have brought disaster upon themselves."

Isaiah 3:9

The interesting thing is that while so many Westerners rush into new age religions, body piercing and occultism, many millions in the tribes mentioned in Africa, South America, Asia and the Pacific islands, are being converted to Christ and are abandoning the body piercing practices of their pagan past.

It is very clear who are the Christians and who are the pagans in these mission fields. The pagans wear little or no clothing and they engage in a variety of body scarification, body piercing and/or tattoos. On the other hand, the Christians are easily identifiable – they wear clothes and they don't engage in any body modification.

"I have been crucified with Christ and I no longer live but Christ lives in me. The life I now live in the body I live by faith in the Son of God Who loved me and gave Himself for me."

Galatians 2:20

Of course, some older people will still have the scars and the holes – testimony of the pagan past before they were converted – but all earrings, eyebrow rings, nose rings and such like have been removed. And their children are free from these pagan disfigurements. It is unheard of in these areas for Christians to voluntarily pierce or tattoo their bodies. In fact, they are shocked when Western men visit them with ponytails and earrings.

"You are the children of the Lord your God. Do not cut yourselves or shave the front of your heads for the dead, for you are a people holy to the Lord your God."
Deuteronomy 14: 1-2

How then can we explain the widespread toleration and even practice of body piercing in far too many Christian Churches and even Bible Colleges and ministries in the West?

"Don't you know that you yourselves are God's temple and that God's Spirit lives in you? If anyone destroys God's temple, God will destroy him; for God's temple is sacred, and you are that temple. Do not deceive yourselves ...."
1 Corinthians 3: 16-18

Generally it starts off by assuming that if an earring is appropriate for a woman, then it is appropriate for men as well. Some women then reasoned that if men were going to wear an earring, then they would wear multiple earrings. And as so many in the world are wearing nose rings, eyebrow rings, belly rings, tongue studs, etc. then why shouldn't we?

"You adulterous people, don't you know that friendship with the world is hatred towards God? Anyone who chooses to be a friend of the world becomes an enemy of God."
James 4:4

As so many Christians have immersed themselves in pagan music, immoral videos and worldly amusements, it should not surprise us that so many of our youth are indistinguishable from their non-Christian friends. The mind-rotting, brain-numbing, soul-destroying trash that fills the ears, eyes and minds of our youth should be sufficient explanation for the backslidden, immoral and un-Christian behaviour, which now even includes professing Christians disfiguring their bodies with pagan piercings.

"There is no fear of God before their eyes."
Romans 3:18

It is time for Youth leaders and Pastors to study what the Scripture teaches on this subject and then to boldly, and without compromise, preach on these passages and call those people who are defiling their bodies to repent. We need to take God's Word seriously.

"Let us purify ourselves from everything that contaminates body and spirit, perfecting holiness out of reverence for God."
2 Corinthians 7:1

"May God Himself, the God of peace, sanctify you through and through. May your whole spirit, soul and body be kept blameless at the coming of our Lord Jesus."
1 Thessalonians 5:23

Chapter 14: Cursed Names

Choosing a name for a child is a very important responsibility. Often parents consider many things when choosing a name for their child. The choice may be to honour a family member or a close friend, or in admiration for a celebrity or a famous person.

Your family name will usually give you a big clue and reveal to you what hidden powers could be operating along your generational lines. I will leave this one to you. I encourage you to dig deeper into your family name. This is what I call spiritual research and it can pay huge dividends.

You will also notice the sad case of some people. While trying to sound smart and sophisticated, they take on names that can lead them straight into the waiting arms of Satan.

A case in point is a lady who changed her name to Lamia. She had no idea what that name really means. Yet she complains something is moving around inside her body. The evil attached to this name attaches itself to people whose names glorify the devil and will refuse to let them go unless the name is changed and revoked.

The name Lamia is also the name of a Female demon who could transform into a serpent monster from a beautiful woman.

God Himself had to change the name of some of the people in the Bible like Abraham and Sarah.

Hélèné Fulton

No longer shall your name be called Abram, but your name shall be Abraham; for I have made you a father of many nations.

Genesis 17:5

Then God said to Abraham, "As for Sarai your wife, you shall not call her name Sarai, but Sarah *shall be* her name.

Genesis 17:15

In other cases, God had to give precise instructions on how people were to be named like John the Baptist and Jesus.

The name given to Jesus was not chosen by Mary and Joseph. His name was chosen by God and told to them before the baby was born. The significance of God's choice is evident in the name. In the gospels, he is called Jesus, but that is the Greek form of his Hebrew name. The gospels were written in Greek because it was the literary language of the time. The Hebrew name of Jesus is Joshua, more properly pronounced Yeshua, which means "The Lord saves" or simply "Saviour".

Similarly, the word, "Christ", is a Greek translation of the Hebrew word, "Mashiakh", which means "Anointed One" or "Messiah". As early as the first century, Jesus was called "Joshua Mashiakh" or "Jesus Christ", not as a title, but as his personal name. We commonly refer to Jesus as Jesus Christ. If we were to call him by his Hebrew name, it would be Joshua Mashiakh. In either language, his name means "Saviour, the Anointed One."

In the ancient, Biblical world, names were important for identity and meaning for the individual as a member of a community. Children were given names by their parents, which were significant to the circumstances of their birth or the destiny of the child. An example is the name, Moses, which in Hebrew means literally 'to draw out'. This is an appropriate name for Moses, who as an infant was saved from death by being drawn out of the water for Pharaoh's daughter. As a man, Moses became the leader of the Hebrew people and led them out of slavery in Egypt to freedom.

Sometimes the name of a person in the Bible changes because of specific circumstances. Saul became an apostle of Jesus to the Gentiles of the Roman Empire, so his name was changed to the Roman name, Paul. Jesus changed the Hebrew name of his disciple, Simon, to the Greek name, Petros, which means 'rock', because Jesus wanted Simon to build a foundation for his mission to the world.

The Damascus Road: Saul Converted
9 Then Saul, still breathing threats and murder against the disciples of the Lord, went to the high priest 2 and asked letters from him to the synagogues of Damascus, so that if he found any who were of the Way, whether men or women, he might bring them bound to Jerusalem.
3 As he journeyed he came near Damascus, and suddenly a light shone around him from heaven. 4 Then he fell to the ground, and heard a voice saying to him, "Saul, Saul, why are you persecuting Me?"
5 And he said, "Who are You, Lord?"

Then the Lord said, "I am Jesus, whom you are persecuting. It *is* hard for you to kick against the goads."

⁶ So he, trembling and astonished, said, "Lord, what do You want me to do?"
Then the Lord *said* to him, "Arise and go into the city, and you will be told what you must do."
⁷ And the men who journeyed with him stood speechless, hearing a voice but seeing no one. ⁸ Then Saul arose from the ground, and when his eyes were opened he saw no one. But they led him by the hand and brought *him* into Damascus. ⁹ And he was three days without sight, and neither ate nor drank.

Ananias Baptizes Saul
¹⁰ Now there was a certain disciple at Damascus named Ananias; and to him the Lord said in a vision, "Ananias."
And he said, "Here I am, Lord."
¹¹ So the Lord *said* to him, "Arise and go to the street called Straight, and inquire at the house of Judas for *one* called Saul of Tarsus, for behold, he is praying. ¹² And in a vision he has seen a man named Ananias coming in and putting *his* hand on him, so that he might receive his sight."
¹³ Then Ananias answered, "Lord, I have heard from many about this man, how much harm he has done to Your saints in Jerusalem. ¹⁴ And here he has authority from the chief priests to bind all who call on Your name."
¹⁵ But the Lord said to him, "Go, for he is a chosen vessel of Mine to bear My name before Gentiles, kings, and the children of Israel. ¹⁶ For I will show him how many things he must suffer for My name's sake."
¹⁷ And Ananias went his way and entered the house; and laying his hands on him he said, "Brother Saul, the Lord Jesus, who appeared to you on the road as you came, has sent me that you may receive your sight and be filled with the Holy Spirit." ¹⁸ Immediately there fell from his eyes *something* like scales, and he received his sight at once; and he arose and was baptized.
¹⁹ So when he had received food, he was strengthened. Then Saul spent some days with the disciples at Damascus.

Witchcraft in the Church

Saul Preaches Christ

[20] Immediately he preached the Christ in the synagogues, that He is the Son of God.

[21] Then all who heard were amazed, and said, "Is this not he who destroyed those who called on this name in Jerusalem, and has come here for that purpose, so that he might bring them bound to the chief priests?"

[22] But Saul increased all the more in strength, and confounded the Jews who dwelt in Damascus, proving that this *Jesus* is the Christ.

Saul Escapes Death

[23] Now after many days were past, the Jews plotted to kill him. [24] But their plot became known to Saul. And they watched the gates day and night, to kill him. [25] Then the disciples took him by night and let *him* down through the wall in a large basket.

Saul at Jerusalem

[26] And when Saul had come to Jerusalem, he tried to join the disciples; but they were all afraid of him, and did not believe that he was a disciple. [27] But Barnabas took him and brought *him* to the apostles. And he declared to them how he had seen the Lord on the road, and that He had spoken to him, and how he had preached boldly at Damascus in the name of Jesus. [28] So he was with them at Jerusalem, coming in and going out. [29] And he spoke boldly in the name of the Lord Jesus and disputed against the Hellenists, but they attempted to kill him. [30] When the brethren found out, they brought him down to Caesarea and sent him out to Tarsus.

The Church Prospers

[31] Then the churches throughout all Judea, Galilee, and Samaria had peace and were edified. And walking in the fear of the Lord and in the comfort of the Holy Spirit, they were multiplied.

Aeneas Healed

[32] Now it came to pass, as Peter went through all *parts of the country*, that he also came down to the saints who dwelt in Lydda. [33] There he found a certain man named Aeneas, who had been bedridden eight years and was paralyzed. [34] And Peter said to him, "Aeneas, Jesus the Christ heals you. Arise and make your bed." Then he arose immediately. [35] So all who dwelt at Lydda and Sharon saw him and turned to the Lord.

Dorcas Restored to Life

[36] At Joppa there was a certain disciple named Tabitha, which is translated Dorcas. This woman was full of good works and charitable deeds which she did. [37] But it happened in those days that she became sick and died. When they had washed her, they laid *her* in an upper room. [38] And since Lydda was near Joppa, and the disciples had heard that Peter was there, they sent two men to him, imploring *him* not to delay in coming to them. [39] Then Peter arose and went with them. When he had come, they brought *him* to the upper room. And all the widows stood by him weeping, showing the tunics and garments which Dorcas had made while she was with them. [40] But Peter put them all out, and knelt down and prayed. And turning to the body he said, "Tabitha, arise." And she opened her eyes, and when she saw Peter she sat up. [41] Then he gave her *his* hand and lifted her up; and when he had called the saints and widows, he presented her alive. [42] And it became known throughout all Joppa, and many believed on the Lord. [43] So it was that he stayed many days in Joppa with Simon, a tanner.

Acts 9

Let me tell you about Elizabeth (meaning oath of God or I am God's or God's promise) and how an occultic maid told her mother to change her name to Lindiwe (meaning to wait) which put a curse on her. Lindiwe came to us in 2011 and could not understand why their business is not doing well and why she always had pains all over her body. Lindiwe was in her 50's when she came to see us. God showed us that she was always playing at a canteen like place but the people around her were very occultic. Very evil and they did not like her much. Lindiwe confirmed this vision that God showed us. They stayed in a mine village and the maid that was taking care of her always took her to the "canteen" which is sort of like a restaurant for all the mineworkers. She also remembers that it was this maid that said that her mother must call her Lindiwe instead of Elizabeth. She also remembers how this maid always said to her mother that she will not become a "big or famous person" with a name like Elizabeth.

The curse was immediately broken including all the curses spoken over Lindiwe by using the prayer below. God also said that she must immediately change her name back and make sure everyone calls her by her real name Elizabeth.

Do a google search to find out the meaning of your name. This includes any nick names given to you.

Prayer
In the name of Jesus Christ I confess all the sins of my forefathers, and by the redemptive blood of Jesus, I now break the power of every curse passed down to me through my ancestral line. I confess and repent of each and every sin that I have committed, known or unknown, and accept Christ's forgiveness. He has redeemed me from the curse of the law. I choose the blessing and reject the curse. In the name of my Lord Jesus Christ, I break the power of every evil curse spoken against me. I cancel the force of every prediction spoken about me, whether intentionally or carelessly, that was not according to God's promised blessings. I bless those who have cursed me. I forgive each person who has

ever wronged me or spoken evil of me. In the name of Jesus Christ, I command every evil spirit of curse to leave me now. Amen.

In Daniel 10, Daniel prayed and fasted for 21 days. God heard his prayer but the devil also heard Daniel praying, and he took adequate measures to see that Daniel's answer did not come or at least he tried.

¹¹ And he said to me, "O Daniel, man greatly beloved, understand the words that I speak to you, and stand upright, for I have now been sent to you." While he was speaking this word to me, I stood trembling. ¹² Then he said to me, "Do not fear, Daniel, for from the first day that you set your heart to understand, and to humble yourself before your God, your words were heard; and I have come because of your words. ¹³ But the prince of the kingdom of Persia withstood me twenty-one days; and behold, Michael, one of the chief princes, came to help me, for I had been left alone there with the kings of Persia.

Daniel 10:11-13

This scripture is a huge eye opener. We can see that Daniel prayed and fasted for three weeks. Right from day one God supplied the answer. But there was a satanic immigration officer in the second heaven, fighting to prevent Daniel from getting the answer.

So one of God's chief angels had to be sent in order for the answer to be released.

This is why prayer is hard work. Your prayer must be sharp enough to go up and pass the second heaven.

Your prayer must be violent enough to penetrate the second heaven to bring down the answer.

Witchcraft in the Church

The powers in the second heaven can hinder prayers. Imagine the battles in the heavens for three weeks.

Heavenly battles normally precede our victory here on earth

Daniel's continuous prayer bombardment reinforced the heavenly army. If Daniel had not been serious with his prayer the answer would not have come.

You might ask, "Why did God not send a powerful angel to immediately bring the answers to Daniel?"

Now look at this carefully.

Your life determines the kind of angels that will be sent to you when you pray. If you are not living in any known sin, and your prayer is continuous and violent, violent and unstoppable angels will bring your answers.

The second thing that will determine what kind of angel comes to your aid has to do with the foothold of the enemy in your life.

In Daniel's case, perhaps the reason he had any problem was not because of sin. He was a very godly man. I think it was because when he got to Babylon as a captive, his name was changed to "Belteshazzar," which was the name of an idol. That idol could get up and argue because he was bearing their name!

What we do know is that when the enemy wanted to come against Elisha, they failed. The purity and violent nature of Elisha, who had a double portion of anointing, made it impossible for soldiers to arrest him.

The Bible says there were horses and chariots of fire surrounding him.

So anytime he wanted to carry a message to heaven, horses and chariots of fire would carry it swiftly! No power could stop him.

Everything that comes to us from God has to cross the second heaven and everything going to God from here goes through there too. It is like a spiritual border or immigration posts with demonic customs and demonic immigration officers.

It is at this point that the strongman in charge of our families, towns and places of birth operate.

We have special teachings in our Prayer Academy to teach you and equip you to resist the devil. Our teaching will also guarantee you that personal relationship with God that you desire. For more on this visit www.prayeracademy.co.za.

Chapter 15: Witchcraft

Witchcraft is the practice of magic and praying or worshipping anything or anyone other than God the Father, God the Son and God the Holy Spirit.

Poisoned by witchcraft

During 2009 Jacob asked his mother to cook for us every night as I had a huge website to design and with my other work, I was sometimes still busy in the early morning hours.

After about 3 days I started developing a burning feeling in my stomach. I asked Jacob's mother if she is adding something to her food that might cause my stomach to burn. She said she put tomatoes and garlic in every meal. I knew this could not be the problem as I eat lots of tomatoes and garlic and never had a problem before.

A week later I was so ill I could not climb two steps. I would wake up and go to the bathroom across the passage and then be too tired to go back. I was dizzy and so weak I could not walk 4 steps without wanting to collapse.

Another week went by and I was taken to the doctor by my son. After a lot of tests including blood tests, the doctor said he could not find anything wrong with me physically

I clearly heard a voice saying this is not from God you are being poisoned.

On my return home I told Jacob's mother that I will from that moment prepare our own food. My son started cooking for us as I was too weak. 3 Days later I was my old self again.

Jacob continued to eat at his mother's place most of the nights and every morning he would go and drink coffee with his father and eat porridge at his parents place.

I felt that every time I had coffee at their place I could not concentrate and I could not focus on Bible study or my prayers. I would start praying and then after a sentence forget what I was asking. I stopped drinking coffee at his mother's place.

These are people who do not miss a church service. They are in the New Apostolic church, but yet they wanted to poison me by be-witching the food and the coffee. Why? To stop me from spreading the Word of God.

Killed by witchcraft

This is a testimony from one of my spiritual daughters.

I have to get something off my chest. The last Prayer Academy lesson we got really got to me. My mother was involved in consulting with Sangomas when I was much younger (Primary School). She had a business from home and regularly went to buy "[18]muti" to increase her profits. The helper at our home was also some sort of medium – she could read the future with tea leaves and

---

[18] Muti is another word for potion.

Witchcraft in the Church

such. My mother and I was very close and so she told me what she did. I didn't know much about this stuff so I saw nothing wrong with it. My mother was always burning stuff in the house and putting on creams and stuff on her body. She also consulted with them about the children (me and my two sisters and brother). I don't know if she ever gave us something, but I am not discarding the option. I remember her telling me the one time that the Sangoma told her that he could only see three children and my mother kept on telling him that she had four. She didn't want to tell me who it was. Over the years I have thought about it a lot trying to figure out what it could mean – I don't know why really. At first I believed that it was due to the fact that she signed off my baby sister into the care of her boyfriend's parents. Then my brother got severe epileptic attacks and the doctors told us that he wouldn't live long because we discovered it too late and his brain has been damaged a lot, so I then thought that was a possible reason. Now I am thinking that God was protecting me from them and that they couldn't see me because I was under the blood. Even though I didn't know much back then, I always used to ask God to protect me and to cover me under the blood of Jesus even though I myself didn't understand the power of the blood of Jesus.

My mother also hated my father. He drank a lot and then abused her. My mother used to wish he would die so she can be free from the heartache and difficulty. My dad did give us a hard time. We were in constant fear of him. I believe that he was possessed by demons and sometimes they would manifest and he would do strange things. I was 16 when my dad passed away. But his death came suddenly and strangely. A year before his

Hélèné Fulton

death somewhere in October my mother came to me and said that the medium told her that my father was going to die in November of that year – it was the same year my dad started smuggling with diamonds. I was shocked and didn't want it to be true and was scared that one of the diamond deals would go bad, so I prayed that God would protect him and help him with his problem. My father lived a year longer, but passed away Christmas day the next year.

A week before my dad got very ill. Something that we have never seen before. I just didn't get up from bed. And the whole week we try to take him to the doctor, but he refused saying it almost Christmas no one is going to help him. Well Christmas day came and he was really sick, to a point that we phoned an Ambulance to come get him. I was the only person who did not want to go to the hospital so I stayed behind, but I could feel something wasn't right. I felt a presence in the house and everywhere around me. I tried to keep myself busy with stuff so I wouldn't think about it. Later that evening my mother came home crying. She didn't want to tell us what happened. She kept on saying, "I'm sorry". I couldn't understand for what. Then one of my parents' home friends came over. My mother asked him to break the news to us. My sister being 14 at that stage tried to tell the doctor that they my father's heart stopped beating, but they ignored her, because what does she know. Today I am convinced the Holy Spirit told her. Eventually later on they realised his heart stopped about three times before his body went into shock and then his insides burst.

Looking back at everything, I now believe that my mother "killed" my dad, why else would she have said that she was sorry – a normal person's reactions would have been "why did it happen, I don't understand".

Witchcraft in the Church

I am not sad about what happened anymore. I am not mad at my mother for doing what she did, but I do however have a concern about all of the curses that was placed on us because of what she did.

This mother called herself a Christian and was brought up in the NG Church. She even married a pastor from a Charismatic Church after this. A Prophet prophesying in this church and said that this church walls will come down if they do not stop offering their children to mammon. This prophecy came true within 3 years. The women and the pastor divorced and he is in his 6th marriage. He already had 3 heart attacks.

I renounce God and I wanted to die

As I remember my childhood I was very withdrawn, I didn't like to be around too much people because I had a very low self-esteem, I believed I was ugly and no one could tell me different. I started getting visitations at the age of 5, from what I can remember, I used to share a room with my older sister who most times was at my grannies place especially holidays and weekends. My younger sister was a baby and needed my parents attention more. I love my parents dearly and believed they did their best they possibly could to raise us.

Anyway I was paralyzed with fear every time I had to go to bed and my mom always closed the door and the light was always off, that's when fear crept in. I would sleep with blankets completely over my head no matter how hot it was! I could hear these things and sometimes see them. My tummy would turn and sometimes they would slowly pull the covers off from me and this went on for a long time.

My parents didn't believe me they just thought I was a scared and nervous child and because I had a bladder problem too, I would wet bed most nights until the age of 10years.
This one night as I was laying in bed with covers over me, holding the blanket so tight and the sweat dripping, with tears in my eyes, I felt a lifting of the blanket and this lady slowly came towards me with a smirk on her face. She had short black hair, moles on her face, a yellow top with black polka dots and red long nails and she stretched her hands towards me saying I must go with her. I was beyond scared and couldn't move. Eventually she disappeared. I will never forget that night, it's still so clear to me.

As I grew up I was drawn into the darker things like horror movies, Stephen King and Dean R Koonts books. I used to enjoy dark stories. My group of friends in primary school used to entertain each other with scary stories. I couldn't understand why I craved for it yet I was so very scared and overwhelmed with fear!

In high school I got deeper into occultic books, religious books, witchcraft, voodoo...I just read anything that was scary and search for things people couldn't explain to me. I would listen to rock heavy metal and thrash metal music, it gave me somewhat boldness and I liked it! At this time I didn't know Jesus. I heard about Him, was given religious lessons in school about Him, but I thought He was a myth. I thought there is no way He could be real. I knew absolutely nothing about Him, the cross, His life or anything about Him. My parents attended church on occasions like funerals and

Witchcraft in the Church

functions and when I would go with my mom, it was Afrikaans and I barely understood it. Mom was Old Apostolic and Dad was Anglican.
Anyway, I started searching for answers in books which I couldn't find, I said to myself that somewhere in here there should be a God? I would look around at stars, clouds and think someone had to create this, but who? And where is He? By this time my depression got deeper, I started writing poetry. I would watch people perform the same things over and over every day, same old patterns every day! Was it worth it? And I thought I don't want that maybe I should just die, kill myself.... life was too depressing I had an indescribable void inside me. I would see how people struggled, how women are abused, how children were hurt and it would keep me up at night and I would think about it all the time and cry myself to sleep. Where is God???!!!

Then one of my friends got hold of a satanic book and I read it, on my 16th birthday. Mom and dad gave me a special party for my friends and I felt special. That's when I got a glimpse of my daughter's father. He helped decorate our yard, and I thought he was handsome but was way too old and I left it there!

My friend who gave me the books came that evening and wanted to take me to a satanic church.

I thought why? It's my birthday, how weird!! I refused thinking they're weird. During my teenage years I pretty much rebelled like other teenagers but I was deeper than them. I saw things differently. I would also see things that no one else could see, hear things no one else would hear.

Hélèné Fulton

I would sit for hours in my room and stare blankly because I had so many thoughts to entertain me. I drank lots of alcohol, experimented with dagga, started cutting myself, renounced God, because in this book my friend gave me you have to say prayers almost like the sinners prayer. Because I was ignorant and thought it won't work, I did it. I played [19]witchy board,[20]glassie glassie, had pictures of mass murderers in my cupboard and attempted suicide a few times and one time nearly succeeded if it wasn't for God. The elders of my dad's friend's church interceded for me. I took an overdose of gout tablets, alcohol and was at home. I woke up, no one knew what I done. I told my mum and she got people to rush me to hospital. All hospitals refused me. Mom half carrying me from hospital to hospital with the neighbour's car and me being too weak and vomiting non-stop. It was traumatic for my mom, they brought me home but there was no one to help me. By then I should've been dead. My grandparents came down and other family members searched for a hospital for me. While I was in bed and my mum was feeding me not knowing what to do, they eventually got to a private hospital on their medical aid that doesn't cover suicide so I had to first go to one of the filthiest and gang infested hospitals to drink charcoal then get treated at the private hospital and my parents couldn't stay. I had to endure the dirty clothes of blood and faeces, the pain, all my muscles stopped working.

---

[19]The Ouija board (/ˈwiːdʒə/ WEE-jə) also known as a spirit board or talking board, is a flat board marked with the letters of the alphabet, the numbers 0-9, the words "yes", "no", "hello" (occasionally), and "goodbye", along with various symbols and graphics. It uses a planchette (small heart-shaped piece of wood) or movable indicator to indicate the spirit's message by spelling it out on the board during a séance. Participants place their fingers on the planchette, and it is moved about the board to spell out words.
[20]This is just another version of the Ouija board

Witchcraft in the Church

Eventually my dad took me to private hospital, where I was poked with needles the whole day, all day. I looked bad, very bad, almost like death. I had fits, lumber puncture, I couldn't eat, couldn't move. Whenever I saw my parents or my siblings they would burst into tears. I had so many doctors, professors their children, even student doctors came to look at me; my body was filled with soars.

I was hopeless, I cried all the time. When my parents were not there I would phone and just cry all day long. That time I had a boyfriend, who today is the father of my 13 year old daughter; he is still a part of my life. I had another fit, then a cat scan. When I woke up in a private room my grandparents, sisters and parents where all crying and looking at me. I knew this was it, my body couldn't take the pain, all my organs were messed up and I had no energy. I made peace with death and said if there is a God I'm ready, I didn't care what happened. I was enough of a burden to my parents and the pain was unbearable!

Then after many tests I started getting a little stronger.

I was laying in intensive care and no one could touch me. I had to wear a mask when visitors came. My boyfriend was not allowed to touch me, like kiss or hold my hand etc. because I could catch germs, so after week or so I started to heal. Dad and mom's life stopped there. It now revolved around me, my younger sister was 14 years old and older sister was 22 and I was 18, just matriculated. Dad took me for physiotherapy and everything else while I was in hospital. They barely went home. I started healing and doctors couldn't believe it, they were shocked when I walked out.

My hair fell out completely and new hair was already growing under old hair. All the filth in my body surfaced on the outside, yes I looked terrible but I was healing.

That was the start of a new journey, as God watched over me and people He assigned to pray for me. He waited and waited for me as it was a few years after that, that I received my salvation. His patience is amazing.

He never gave up on me. When I came out of hospital my hair started growing slowly, I had to rest a lot. I could not receive many visitors and never went out because I looked terrible. My boyfriend came every now and then and I preferred it like that.

Then I had to go to a psychiatrist and mom and dad took me every week which was expensive. Afterwards I found out how much in debt my parents were and I hated myself for that. I thought I could've just died than to put them all through this heavy financial burden, even my sisters had to feel the loss.

Months passed and I got a job in a clothing store. I started drinking and smoking, soon things went back to normal. I then fell pregnant at the age of 20.

Yes my parents were shocked but they supported me so did the father of the child. I had a heavy fear that I might not carry my child to full term. I was so worried because of the damage to my body, the fear was crippling but my boyfriend kept me positive and I went for regular check-ups.

Witchcraft in the Church

The depression started again. I would cry almost every night in the bath, asking God why He kept me alive. What is the real purpose of life? Eventually I gave birth, had an emergency epidural caesarean and I had a healthy baby girl.

God blessed me once again, she is so precious!

She was now my reason for living. Me and mom encountered a few problems, we argued a lot. I got depressed a lot and preferred to stayed in my room with baby and would just lay with her and cry all the time.

Eventually I looked for work months later, mom looked after my baby. It was contract jobs just for money. My 21st came; it was nice - just intimate family.

Then as time went on me and boyfriend had a lot of arguments, financial issues and we both drank, by then my daughter was 2years old. I placed her in a crèche and I started studying early childhood development. Then as time went on my boyfriend had to be best man for his cousins wedding and the cousin bought him a ticket to Germany because he lived there. He didn't want to go but I persuaded him because I would be fine and Diana was too young to go.

The same night he left, things started to happen, it was during the December holidays.
That same night after we took him to the airport something came into my room, a big shadow but just before it came I saw my late grandpa and he looked down on me then disappeared and this shadowy thing choked me. For more than a month these things came

Hélèné Fulton

every night to me in different shapes, forms, colours etc. always after 5am choking, scratching, pressing me, seducing me. At first my parents thought it was my imagination but it got serious. Every night my sisters would take turns to sleep by me or me by them and then my parents and I always use to beg them not to let me fall asleep because as soon as it happened they attacked. But the thing is when they shook me and choked me, my bed shook but my daughter was always lying next to me unharmed and she was about 3 years old and a light sleeper but never woke up, she slept peacefully. We tried different methods. Religious stuff to get rid of these things, nothing worked. 3 weeks later my boyfriend came from Germany. He moved in for a while because of problems with siblings, his parents are deceased, mom said fine as long as he brought his own bed. By that time things got hectic, we were lying one evening on the bed talking. Him holding me then something pushed me away from him. Then he could see himself what was happening but still he didn't believe. Different people tried to help, telling me to give my life to the Lord and I refused. They told me it will come back in sevens. I didn't really understand much, one of the people that prayed for me and on me from this Christian church told me the vision he saw. He said he saw me stand at a rally speaking to lots of people and I had a mic in my hand and they were crying as I spoke and the other thing is there was a certain bruise on my arm, not a lot of people knew about it and Holy Spirit showed him that too and you can't easily see it. So they prayed and anointed my room and the entire house and everyone in it. They said I should sleep peacefully. So I did that night, yes the next night it came back!

I told my mom's friend about it because she knew about everything and she's a prayer warrior and she said I must come over and she prayed and prayed and the thing left.

Witchcraft in the Church

After that I slept well. For me everything was fine, bad things must happen. I always looked for excuses for certain things. I eventually worked at a different day care centre, and then I ended up at the school that I am presently, a primary school, this is my 6th year. The first year I got there I had a student teacher who shadowed me. She was saved, blood washed, so humble and always smiling. I didn't want to get too close to her because I was scared she might preach to me.

So slowly but surely she showed me books she was reading and explaining to me about Jesus and Holy Spirit. I started to become interested in it and I read a few books and I thought wow maybe there really is a God. At the same time my younger sister was also going through the same thing with someone at her work that was feeding her the word and explaining to her and sometimes I would see her reading the bible.

Then this lady would feed me bit by bit and I would ask her hundreds of questions. I eventually I told her what happened when this demonic force was after me and she explained. I told her it's happening again that I have insomnia and gets rushes of depression sometimes. I told her I feel so heavy like something is on my back, she said she will speak to this counsellor who is a prophet, it's an old lady who helped many and she trusted her with her life and I said yes. I went on the Saturday.

That was when my life changed. I went to her with this friend, it was full of pastors and elders, and they were chatting and introduced me. She asked if I wanted to talk alone with her, I said yes, so we went to a room and I

didn't say much, the Holy Spirit showed her. I couldn't believe it because no one knew those stuff and then doubt crept in and I just left it there. She started getting heavy nausea and started to cry and she scared me. I thought oh my goodness what did this
God show her. She saw an upside down cross and many other things.

She told me how much Jesus loved me and the plan He has for me and she just started ministering to me. I felt something bubbling inside me that wanted to come out like a geyser trying to burst and I saw this man on a cross for me. I burst out crying and gave my heart to the Lord.

Eventually I got home, told my parents and they just looked at me. I told my sister and she just smiled. At that time she also gave her heart to the Lord, she just didn't tell anyone. So I went home to my daughter and boyfriend because I lived with them. I got there and they were drinking, I told them what happened and they looked confused and offered me alcohol.

That whole week friends and family visited with alcohol, red wine and ciders because they knew it was my favourite.

It was hard. I had no church. I had no one to direct me and help me teach me. I still didn't know right from wrong, but slowly God directed people my way, He was teaching me. I got CD's to listen to, books to read, then I joined the church I'm at now. I did a disciple course and I got baptized and God lead the way. He gave me lots of dreams and visions to show me things and I realized how much He loves me and that He was always there. That I shouldn't trust my feelings, that He is in control - even as a sinner, when I took those tablets I should have died and gone to hell but His servants prayed

Witchcraft in the Church

for me. When I came out of hospital that time, I met them and they wanted to anoint me. They cried and cried and said the gifts God placed inside me and that God has given me a second chance, that many don't get a second chance and after all that, I went back to my old life and did the same things only to receive Jesus Christ years later.

God never gave up on me, He waited and waited, He never stopped loving me; it was hard to believe after all the rejection and all the bad things I had done. No matter what happens, God finishes what he starts. He is always faithful. I still go through so many dark tunnels but it's hard if you are in a dark place where you can't breathe, where you don't want advice or listen to preaching, I just remember what He has done for me and where I am today. Yes I'm struggling but I know God is working in me to take that muck and residue out, He is watching over me because He loves me. As much as I thought I was a mistake, I always remember that I was conceived in Gods mind before creation and He knew everything before I was born and nothing I do will let Him love me less, although Satan comes and condemns and bring to remembrance the past and we are only human. I force myself to press forward. Today my 13 year old daughter is saved and also a dreamer and has a prophetic calling on her but I always have to cover her, both my sisters are saved and I'm believing for my parents and daughters fathers salvation, the devil used him a lot to bring me down and break me.

But To God all the Glory!!!

Hélèné Fulton

This young lady also experienced her 3rd eye opening and operating during the times she was reading books of the occult. The 3rd eye is now closed as this is demonic and not from God.

She is now 33 and although she is still experiencing attacks, she is doing so much better. She is helping out the youth and other young people in her community.

A cry for help

On 14 December 2011 I received this email.

My name is Sengen McDonald. I live in the Philippines. 13 years ago I came to the Philipines with a missionary on a 21 day trip. When I went back home I started asking God if that is what he wanted me to do. I prayed about it for a long time. I knew that is what He wanted me to do. After talking to my wife and to the church we took the big step and sold all we had and move to the Philippines. My Father was a Evangelist and all my life I was told that I was called by God also. We were doing great. We were doing small and large Crusades with many people receiving Christ and a good healing ministry. At that time all the love that I had for God and my wife was through knowledge. What I know that I should do to be a good husband and to be a good Evangelist how to preach the word of God for people to receive Christ and how to get people healed. My wife and I start having problems and they got bigger and bigger and then it got in to ministry. It became to much for us and I decided I was going to find some where else to live for a while. Then I met a lady that helped me to forget all my problems and that produced a son. My wife and I had no children and she did not want any. She wanted only me in her house. It came down to my only son or my wife and the ministry. I chose my son! I lost

Witchcraft in the Church

everthing. My wife my ministry and all my friends for what I had done. I even gave up on God because I thought I had done the worse thing that I could do to Him and the Church by getting in sin and choosing my son over the ministry. Through the love that I have found for my children I now know how to love my father GOD. I know have a true relationship from my heart not my head. I am now closer to my father God than I have ever been in my life. My deepest desire is to fix my problems and go back to doing what God has called me to do. My wife says now I can have the divorce . But it is all up to me. I have not paid my visa in five years. I can not get a job and I can not leave the country at the risk of not being able to see my children again. I was getting help from my mother but she does not have it any more. I was also getting help from a home church in NC. but they have now split up. I now have no one to ask for help. We are now selling whatever any one will buy out of the house to get rice. This is a plea from the heart to any one to help me and my children. Please take this letter and pray over it and do what God wants you to do.

My reply to Sengen

I do not have money to give you but I can give you the following Prayers that needs to be prayed at Midnight until you get a breakthrough. You have sinned and need to ask God for forgiveness and accept Him once again into your heart.

Start a small service from your house and start teaching the people about God's love. I will sign you up as an evangelist for Light the World Ministries not because you asked because I was told by Father God.

Hélèné Fulton

I know it is difficult but just like Job, God will restore everything satan has taken from you.

You need to get that divorce finalized and marry the women you are living with as this is also a sin in God's eyes.

Make sure that the mother of your children have 100% the same faith as you otherwise she will open doorways for satan to attack you.

He replied back on 16 December 2013

I read your e-mail again. Like I said I confess daily over my life and my problem. I have 7 books on Charles Capps. I even have his confession book. I also preach from time to time. I do not know how yet but when the righteous cry the Lord hears and does deliver them. Job 36 tells me that I am still on the thorne with Kings but tied in fenders. (My feet are bond) So are my hands until I get help!!!!. I am sending my e-mail to ever one I can find. I pray that it will get in to the right hands. I have all my TRUST in God!!!

My response:

I have given you specific prayers to break the things that is upon you. It seems like you are not taken the word of a Prophet of God seriously. I have been anointed by God Himself as His Prophet and before every answer to you I have asked God to give me the answer. Your e-mail did get to the right hands and you have receive exactly what you need to do but yet you still do not listen. You wanted help from God but expected it in money. Take your own flesh out and start working for God the way you should be according to God and not the way you think you should with your flesh.

Witchcraft in the Church

Start a home church and a bible study group from your house. Ask the people that come to bring their own chairs.

Outcome:

Sengen are currently running a bible study group, youth centre and a home church from his house and it is going great with him and his family. Dying to that old self and listening to God is the first step to prosperity and setting the captives free.

In Rebellion

19 December 2012

I was in a relationship for 12 years with my first and only boyfriend whom I got married to on the 18th of December 2010 and we had a baby girl who was born in May this year. When my daughter was just 4 weeks, he told me he no longer loves me and moved out. We were a God fearing couple, very much in love and building a great future together. I had prayed for a husband and truly believed this was the one and yet that's not the case? We work in the same building I see him every day and we don't communicate instead we communicate via my lawyer whom I contacted and asked to proceed with divorce. We are at the called to sign the settlement agreement stage if he is not going to contest the divorce. It's just weird the whole thing and how quickly things fell apart and it have left me faithless - why didn't God hear my prayers? It feels too late to restore anything and quite frankly crazy to go back. What does God want for my life? I have attached a picture of my daughter and what was my life. I'm now backsliding and I feel far from God, very far.

Please help if you can. Elsie

As always when I get a request for help I take it to Father God for the answer.

My response:

Get back in line with God then He will answer your prayers. Also you need to remember if this is not the man that God wants for you God will rather send another good man your way.

But why allow me to marry him, have a child with him if he isn't the one that God wanted for me? Praying becomes a futile exercise. What's the use of getting back in line with the very same God I prayed to for a husband and when Satan came to rob and steal I still prayed to God and He did nothing. I have been a Christian all my life but I have never felt so let down by God which is why I have backslidden and actually have zero faith, zero. Life makes no sense.

Thank you though. Elsie

Sometimes when I am busy helping people under the guidance of the Holy Spirit I am shocked at what I type or say. But I learnt that God always knows what to say and He knows what has happened and will happen in that person's life. So I trust God completely. He has never let me down and never will.

Witchcraft in the Church

My response:
God never said you must marry him. You did this because this is what you wanted. If you have asked God that time and listen to Him you would not have married him. I think you need to sit down and think hard how many people actually warned you before you got married.

Prophet Helene,

I wish I could agree with you but I don't. I truly believed that this is what God wanted for my life. I dedicated so much prayer. Yes, there were a few voices against this marriage, this was placed in God's hands and many people prayed over this decision - many. This is why I am so lost, what is the point of praying and fasting - what is the point of corporate prayer? What is the point of the prayer of agreement if when you are convinced that you have heard from God it actually isn't His will or His voice? What a waste of 12 years. What a letdown of my faith. And let's pretend for one minute, it was me - is God not so mighty and loving that He would close the door prior to me getting married if He knew all this is not what He wanted for me? I was engaged for a whole 2 years where I sought God's voice. I prayed. I put out a fleece. I fasted. I got engaged in 2008 and only got married in 2010.

I don't know how to believe God when He says He has a plan for my life? What plan? To guide me on a path where He gives and takes away? What's the point of believing if what will be will be any way? I am beyond broken. I am completely shattered because everything I thought was, wasn't and now I am left to redefine what actually is. God knows what I will tell my daughter one day because I really don't know. Elsie

Once again I was shocked by the way God had me answer this lady.

My response:

You are in rebellion.

[22] And Samuel said, Hath the Lord as great delight in burnt offerings and sacrifices, as in obeying the voice of the Lord? Behold, to obey is better than sacrifice, and to hearken than the fat of rams.
[23] For rebellion is as the sin of witchcraft, and stubbornness is as iniquity and idolatry. Because thou hast rejected the word of the Lord, he hath also rejected thee from being king.

1 Samuel 15:22-23

So make no mistake, God does not take rebellion of any form lightly! No matter what the circumstances, God is offended by rebellion. You have to realise that God does NOT bless rebellion, no matter how much GRACE is on your life!

If all "hell" is breaking loose in your life right now…just maybe it's because you are in rebellion in an area.

You see, we are born into sin. Rebellion is unfortunately rooted in our flesh. Our flesh can be trained as we discipline ourselves towards godliness…but you must never EVER forget the fact that your flesh will always kick and rebel against the things of the Spirit and what God wants for your life! It's up to you on a daily basis to decide… Am I going to rule this flesh… or am I going to allow it to rule me?

Witchcraft in the Church

- When we don't keep the speed limit, that's rebellion
- When we go on compulsive, emotional, shopping sprees, that's rebellion
- When we withdraw, sulk or throw our toy's out the cot, that's rebellion
- When we refuse to tithe, that's rebellion
- When we are stubborn and strong willed, that's rebellion
- When children do not honor and respect their parents that is rebellion
- When you always speak down to others that is rebellion
- When you are racists that is rebellion
- When we are self-focused and self-centered, that's rebellion
- When we criticize, condemn and continually find fault with everything or everyone, that's rebellion
- When you murmur under your breathe or become disgruntled and unappreciative of anything or any of the leadership in your church, that's rebellion
- Anything that you do that is against the moral law or the commandments of God will bring you in rebellion with God.

After reading what my answer to her was, I wondered if I should put it in a different way as it sounded very harsh. Immediately God said send it as it is. I obeyed without asking any further questions as God knows what is best.

I press send and I truly thought that I will never hear from Elsie again. But I did and I was surprised.

Wow. I now understand.
I will do as you say. I will get back in line with God.

Hélèné Fulton

Thank you for being frank and honest. I truly appreciate it.

Please pray for me.

Thank you, Elsie

Jealousy from a mother

During our telephone conversation a statue was revealed that was given as a present and had a curse on. This statue caused marital problems and health issues that eventually lead to Martha having to undergo a full hysterectomy at the very young age of 21.

Good morning Helené,

This morning I am at a loss for words. Last night myself and my husband expected you to call us, to do a prayer, maybe some well wishes, but never what happened to us last night. Surely you could have heard that we've been dumb struck by what was happening to us. You became the utensil in GOD's hand to make me experience a miracle which reinstated everything I've believed in throughout my life. We had receive the blessing of real prophetic work which are something very little Christian's have the privilege to experience in such a direct way.

I want to provide you with some info on the statue. This statue came from my previous marriage which was quite violent and an enormous lie. My ex-husband had affairs since we've been married 8 months and it never stopped. The statue was given to us by his mother who bought it in Namibia from Venda veterans very long ago. I used her for a doorstop and she never received any attention from any of us except when one of us bumped our toes to her. I actually had a huge dislike in her but she served her purpose of keeping the door open so there she stood. That is then the reason why we did not knew it was her at first. When however Graham walked to the kitchen to get the olive oil I followed him and as it was meant to be I bumped into her. I immediately knew that this was what you were talking about.

To us we did not need anything else to convince us that you are a servant of God. There is no way in which you could have known about her. I mean she most definitely was not a normal household item kept by everybody. In fact she will not fit in at any modern household.

The presence of GOD was so enormous that even today I feel so filled up that I have not a single empty space that needs attention. I received the mercy I've been begging for. Since the beginning of our adoption trail I've never felt so secure and at peace. GOD took over our struggle.

I do wish I had the words to properly thank you. You brought us to a level we've never imagined possible. Thank you so much for being such a caring and loving servant of GOD that not even the fact that we are not directly linked to your ministry and strangers to you stopped you from spending your private time on helping us.

To us you are one of the true leaders in GOD's army and an impeccable example of what GOD stand for.

Hélèné Fulton

THANK YOU SO MUCH!!!! May all the good you spread amongst the nation of GOD be returned to you in triple measures.

Enjoy your weekend.

Regards, Martha

They cursed a baby

March 2011 during a crusade, God revealed a person's name while busy with another person. It was the neighbor of the person we was busy praying for.

I ask the person to please tell Hannes to come and see me as soon as possible.

Hannes came the next day with his stepdad as he was too scared to come alone.

God revealed that there were a man and a woman very wealthy and very powerful in his life as a baby. His stepdad then revealed that Hannes was going to be adopted as a baby by two lawyers, but his mother could not go through with the adoption.

God also revealed that these two people were Satanists and that God stopped the adoption.

These two Satanists were so angry that they cursed the baby. When God revealed to me Hannes's name He also revealed to me the curse on the Hannes.

Hannes was not born again but was a devoted Christian. I explained to him what it means to be born again and he

Witchcraft in the Church

accepted Jesus Christ as his Lord and Savior and the curse was broken instantly. Glory to God. Praise His works.

Witchcraft is everywhere. It is on the Television, in the stores, and even in the churches. It is being shamelessly advertised wherever you go.

Just look at the huge sales of the Harry Potter books and movies. This is a triumph for witchcraft in the world as every child wants to be a witch or warlock. Gone are the days when witches used to be old toothless women playing their crafts under the cover of darkness in some obscure corners of the earth or in a dark cave.

Witchcraft has been repackaged to look exciting and glamorous. To draw everyone, especially kids into it. But let's get back to the Bible to examine the true nature of witchcraft.

The Woe of Nineveh
3 Woe to the bloody city!
It *is* all full of lies *and* robbery.
Its victim never departs.
² The noise of a whip
And the noise of rattling wheels,
Of galloping horses,
Of clattering chariots!
³ Horsemen charge with bright sword and glittering spear.
There *is* a multitude of slain,
A great number of bodies,
Countless corpses—
They stumble over the corpses—

Hélèné Fulton

⁴ Because of the multitude of harlotries of the seductive harlot,

The mistress of sorceries,
Who sells nations through her harlotries,
And families through her sorceries.

Nahum 3:1-4

Witchcraft is vicious but highly deceptive. It can sell families, communities and entire nations.

A single person in the family who consults with mediums, astrologers, sorcerers, witches, magicians, false prophets, etc. can open the floodgate of trouble for everyone else in the family.

Through just one visit to anyone working for Satan (anyone in the occult or any pagan religion are working for Satan), the blood of members of the entire family can be sucked and deposited in witchcraft covens! They could even withdraw the organs from the body, leaving people running from pillar to post looking for solutions without finding any.

The result?

Health problems. Business failure. Financial collapse. Marital problems. Drug problems in the family and a bunch of other problems too many to mention here.

When I was down in Burgersfort spreading the Word of God I had a vision of a well-known lady who jumps from church to church and spreads gossip around in town. This lady is in such a rebellion with God. She is also very racist and is trying to run everyone's lives. The vision I saw was of her wearing a mask like the masks some of the African witches sometimes wears.

Witchcraft in the Church

I Never Knew You
²¹ "Not everyone who says to Me, 'Lord, Lord,' shall enter the kingdom of heaven, but he who does the will of My Father in heaven. ²² Many will say to Me in that day, 'Lord, Lord, have we not prophesied in Your name, cast out demons in Your name, and done many wonders in Your name?'
²³ And then I will declare to them, 'I never knew you; depart from Me, you who practice lawlessness!'

Matthew 7:21-23

The Test of Knowing Him
³ Now by this we know that we know Him, if we keep His commandments.

1 John 2:3

¹⁴ Blessed *are* those who do His commandments, that they may have the right to the tree of life, and may enter through the gates into the city.

Revelation 22:14

⁸ The words of a ²¹talebearer *are* like tasty ²²trifles,
And they go down into the inmost body.

Proverbs 18: 8

¹⁶ You shall not go about *as* a talebearer among your people; nor shall you take a stand against the life of your neighbor: I *am* the LORD.

Leviticus 19: 16

In a small town like Burgersfort, young females are stealing business from a god fearing man. A true man of

---
²¹ A person who maliciously gossips or reveals secrets.
²² A Jewish tradition reads *wounds*.

Hélèné Fulton

God by using witchcraft. You know who you are and I know who you are as God revealed this to me. You think just because I am not in Burgersfort God will not show me what you are doing. This after you told me to my face that you just want to do what is right in God's eyes. So what happened to that? To you and your friends that is helping you a small warning. Repent! Ask God for forgiveness for what you have done and never do that again. If not you are facing eternity in hell. And belief me eternity is so long that one will never ever see the end.

Many people say I am a Christian but what they do and how they behave is witchcraft. Do not be one of these people as God will turn away from you.

I have seen many people claiming to be a prophet that use demonic entities to "heal". They take out one problem that was caused by witchcraft sent to you just to make sure you get another. You will only notice this a few days after and will never think about where you got it.

Be careful what you buy, and where you buy it. Never buy anointing oil or "holy water" from anyone as you do not know what that person are doing when the world cannot see him, rather use your authority as a born again believer to prepare your own anointing oil. Contact us at churchoffice@lighttheworldministries.co.za.

Chapter 16: Demonic

The werewolf attack

I was sound asleep when the Holy Spirit woke me up. As I opened my eyes this thing, which looked like a werewolf, with black and brown hair and two rows of metallic teeth - almost gold in colour, attacked me. I could feel the aggression towards me.

I immediately said, "I rebuke you in the name of Jesus". The werewolf left but unfortunately for me one of his teeth caught me next to my nose on my right cheek.

The next morning when I looked in the mirror I had a nasty scratch mark from where the tooth of the werewolf caught me.

From that day on, for several months, every time that Jacob came into my office to say something nasty to me or scream at me, the right side of my face would swell up and I had to put my hand over it and ask God to heal and restore it.

I soon learned that I should bind all words spoken over me the minute Jacob entered my office.

The spiritual world is big and you should ask God to give you discernment.

I remember years ago, two young men working at the Pretoria Zoo as security guards at night, told me that they had seen werewolves. Most people did not believe them.

If you look at some of the movies and series that are on television today you will see that it is very "weird" as they are trying to get the young people to get used to demons and evil spirits in all forms.

Parents should watch what their children are watching.

Imaginary friends

My youngest grandson (3 at the time) was one day talking to a demon disguised as a super hero. His mother said, "Look he has an imaginary friend, how cute". I immediately rebuked her and said that is no imaginary friend. I turned to my grandson and asked him, "Do you think this super hero is from Jesus?" He replied with a NO. Then I told him to tell him to leave. He stood up and very firmly said to the demon, "[23]Voertsek" in the name of Jesus Christ go and never come back you devil.

Remember the child in chapter 9. Soon after she got an imaginary friend she started getting worse.

Some parents will actually set a place at the dinner table so that this demon can eat with them.

Parents teach your children especially the young ones before age 7 to tell you if strange creators or fairies, super heroes or Santa suddenly start visiting them on a regular basis.
Demons will come in any form that is acceptable for a child to that child.

---

[23]An Afrikaans word for telling a dog or animal to go.

In the case of my grandson, demons started to harass him because of his calling. This is also the case of many children. Satan does not want them to step into their calling so he will send someone to distract the child.

Imprinting & Soul ties are the same

Many teenagers are hooked on the Twilight movie and they either wish they could be a Wolf or a Vampire. I recently watched the movie as I was visiting friends and they were watching it. One thing that stood out among the things God pointed out to me was the "imprinting" and how the word "soul ties" are changed by Satan and his co-workers to make it more acceptable to the younger generations. Just like everything else Satan does, he made this look innocent; he made this look like it was to her benefit and safety.

Imprinting & Soul ties are the same thing.

This is how Satan controls you. This is how Satan manipulates you. This is how Satan uses you.

If you are not married and you had sex with someone you need to break the soul ties that was formed between you and the person you had sex with.

[16] Or do you not know that he who is joined to a harlot is one body *with her?* For "the two," He says, "shall become one flesh.
1 Corinthians 6:16

Some of the most popular and destructive soul ties are formed during adultery or fornication. 1 Corinthians 6:16

warns us not to have sexual relations with a prostitute because we become one flesh (flesh as in soul realm kind of flesh, not a physical flesh) with that person. This ungodly soul tie is like a rope between two persons that demons can use to their advantage to cross from one person to another. If that person had demons tormenting them, and you had sex with them, it unites the two persons, and therefore a soul tie is created, and the demons tormenting that person can also have rights to torment you. This does not apply to married couples, because there is no unhealthy soul tie created from sex within marriage. The Bible says that the marriage bed is un-defiled, and defilement is required to create an evil soul tie.

The remedy? Repentance, renunciation and breaking of soul ties! First, specifically repent of the sin which caused the soul tie to be formed in the first place. Then you can use your authority in Jesus to break and sever the unholy soul tie. Saying something like this should do the job, if you have accepted Jesus as your Saviour "I now renounce, break and sever all unholy soul ties created between me and _____ through the act of adultery in Jesus' name!"

There can also be soul ties between yourself and another person, without any sexual relationship involved. Sexual relationships are one of the best ways to create a very strong soul tie, but it's not the only way. Other soul ties can be created through unhealthy relationships, such as being so close to a parent that you take their advice over God's advice. Again, repentance and the breaking of the soul ties in Jesus' name is the way to go about solving this problem.

Another thing that could hold back the breaking of a soul tie, is a physical object given to you from the other person, through a sinful relationship. If you were given a ring, or bra or a love gift through an adulterous relationship, then burn the gift.

Ghosts and a diseased loved one

If you are getting visits from a diseased loved one or someone you knew or a visit from someone who died in the house you live or even smelled like a dead loved one smelled, when he or she was alive, you will be shocked at what I'm about to say.

Demons appear in the form of that person. Rebuke it immediately in the name of Jesus Christ.

I am not saying that this person was demonic. I am saying that Satan wants you to think that it is that person but it is actually a demon posing as that person.

[5] For the living know that they will die;
But the dead know nothing,
And they have no more reward,
For the memory of them is forgotten.
[6] Also their love, their hatred, and their envy have now perished;
Nevermore will they have a share
In anything done under the sun.
Ecclesiastes 9:5-6

These verses prove that the dead do not watch over the living or come back to earth to visit. The dead do not speak through spiritual mediums. These are demons speaking through mediums as mediums are working for the dark kingdom. Satan's kingdom. Yes! Even if they say I am a Christian.

[20] Rather, that the things which the Gentiles sacrifice they sacrifice to demons and not to God, and I do not want you to have fellowship with demons.

1 Corinthians 10:20-21

The dead do not haunt our houses. If your house is "haunted" it is a Territorial spirit. This you can tell to leave with your authority in Christ Jesus. You must be a born again child of God.

The spirits who haunt our houses, call our names, slam doors, turn lights and appliances on or off, appear as fleeting shadows, cause mechanical toys to be set off with or without batteries, speak through spiritual mediums, etc. are not spirits of the dead. They're demonic spirits masquerading as spirits of humans who've died.

The dead do not hang around on earth waiting to be released. The dead do not come back to get you for what you have done or to come and say goodbye. This is not Biblical. It is a false belief perpetuated by psychics and mediums.

There is absolutely no way that these ghosts are truly the spirits of the dead. They're demonic spirits and nothing more.

If you live in a "haunted" house and want to know how to get rid of the spirits who are haunting it please email us.

Alien Abduction

Most people that were "abducted by aliens" believe more in aliens than in God Almighty Himself.

People that are involved in the occult or any form of false doctrine usually experience this. If you are experiencing this and would like to get real help for this then contact us.

Fairies and all other Magical Creatures

We all believed in fairies when we were children and some adults still believe. Just think about some of your favourites like Tinkerbell, the little Mermaid etc. All the girls wanted a fairy godmother like Cinderella. Then there is Santa, who I do not have to say anything about as there is not a person in this world who does not know who Santa is.

Fantasy is still very popular. People collect elves, gnomes, hobbits, and fairies. We love watching Lord of the Rings, Harry Potter, and so forth. Wake-Up people those are very dangerous grounds. All of these 'mystical' beings are demons and they are worshiped in the occult. Disney movies, and fairy tales have made them "cute" but please do not be deceived. Get rid of all these images and collections from your life and out of your home to protect yourself and your family!
Some quotes from many credible sources that will reveal to us the truth about elves, Santa and fairies.

"Fantasy plays an important role in any religious curriculum, for the subjective mind is less discriminating about the quality of its food than it is about the taste. Thus, fantasy is utilized as a magic weapon in Satanism.

Hélèné Fulton

The Satanist maintains a storehouse of avowed fantasy gathered from all cultures and from all ages."

(Anton Szandor LaVey, The Satanic Rituals, p. 15, 27)

*"**Elf**: 'A small, often mischievous creature considered to have magical powers.' Although some of these creatures may appear cute on the surface, all of them are nonetheless demonic entities that have their origin in the occult world."*
(Cathy Burns, Masonic and Occult Symbols Illustrated, p. 77)

"Elf - If a person wants their help, he must apply to their chief, the devil himself. The idea that these spirits are demonic in origin is in accordance with the Bible."
"Goblins and Elves"
(Dr.Kurt Koch, Occult ABC, p. 82, 83)

Elves - "A host of supernatural beings and spirits who exist between earth and heaven.
Fairies or Elves are fallen angels. When God cast Lucifer from heaven, the angels who were loyal to Lucifer plunged down with him."
(Rosemary Ellen Guiley, The Encyclopedia of Witches and Witchcraft, p. 115)

"elves are "disembodied spirits", used in "magic and sorcery" and are "the principal agents in seances."
(H.P. Blavatsky, Isis Unveiled, Vol I, p. 262)

"Modern Christmas elves find their origin in the house gnomes of the Scandinavians, which were present since the pagan times.

Witchcraft in the Church

It was believed that these gnomes guarded homes against evil."

Christmas World; (ABC family)

You only need God to protect you and your family.
"Devil: Besides the name Satan, he is also called Beelzebub, Lucifer and in popular or rustic speech by many familiar terms such as Old Nick."

(Oxford English Dictionary Volume III D-E)

I remember that in December 2011 my grandson (aged 5 at the time) had two weeks of dreams of Santa. It was different dreams but in the end the message was very clear. Santa was telling him that he needs to serve him (Santa) otherwise he will not get a Christmas present. Every morning we broke and cancelled the dream. On day 3 I wrote the name Santa on a piece of paper and during the second week my eye caught the piece of paper on my desk that I totally forgot about and I noticed that the letters in Satan was just scrambled around a bit to form Santa.

"Old Nick: "A well-known British name of the Devil. It seems probable that this name is derived from the Dutch Nikken, which means the devil..."
(Encyclopaedia of Occultism and Parapsychology, p.650)

"(Saint Nick) or "Ole Nick" is listed among the fallen angels or devils in the Dictionary of Fallen Angels. December 25 is actually "the feast in honor of the birth of the son of the Babylonian queen of heaven, later called Saturnaha by the heathen Romans."

(Gail Riplinger, New Age Versions, p. 52)

Hélèné Fulton

"This time of year was in many ways for the Germanic peoples what Samhain was to the Celtics, a time when magic went out into the world, freeing the dead to walk and elves, trolls, gnomes, et cetera were free to roam."
    Santa Claus, the Yule Elf, and Odin by Kimberly Moore.

"In these plays, the devil's common entry line, known as the "devil's bluster," was "Ho! Ho! Ho!"
(Siefker, Phyllis. Santa Claus, Last of the Wild Men: The Origins and Evolution of Saint Nicholas. Jfferson: McFarland & Company, Inc., 1997, p. 69)

"Old Nick - NOUN, the devil or satan - The American Heritage® Dictionary of the English Language: Fourth Edition. 2000

Fairies have a long and winding history in witchcraft and the occult. The Woman's Dictionary of Symbols and Sacred Objects describes the fairy as, "tiny female spirit with butterfly wings. . ." (p. 246) the fairy is depicted as a Queen with a crown. (p. 245) it goes on to say, ". . . the fairies were originally the souls of the pagan dead. . . In several folk ballads the Fairy Queen is addressed as 'Queen of Heaven'. . . Christian sources depicted fairies as real people, almost synonymous with witches."
    (The Woman's Dictionary of Symbols and Sacred Objects, p. 246)

"According to theory, fairies are either: earthbound unbaptized souls; guardians of the souls of the dead; ghosts of venerated ancestors; fallen angels condemned to remain on earth; nature spirits, or small human beings. They are

Witchcraft in the Church

said to have magical powers and to consort with witches and other humans with supernatural powers. . ."
(Geddes and Grosett, Guide to the Occult and Mysticism, p. 446)

The popular Encyclopeadia of Occultism by Lewis Spence, connects fairies to the devil and says of fairies, "They steal human children, and leave in their places fairy changelings..."
(Lewis Spence, Encyclopaedia of Occultism, p. 154)

"In Ireland, all the [24]sidh or fairy hills (grave mounds) were said to open up on the occasion [Halloween]. Folks insisted that it was impossible to keep the fairies underground on Halloween. Since these fairies were simply pagan spirits, the church naturally insisted that demons were abroad on Halloween."
(Walker, Barbara, The Woman's Dictionary of Symbols and Sacred Objects, p. 180)

"If a person wants their [fairies] help, he must apply to their chief, the devil himself. This however, would cost a person his salvation. The idea that these spirits [fairies] are demonic is in accordance with the Bible."
(Dr. Kurt Koch, Occult ABC, p. 83)

According to The Encyclopaedia of Witches and Witchcraft, "Fairies are fallen angels." It goes on to describe fairies as, "Some fairies were said to suck human blood like vampires. Many contemporary Witches believe in fairies and some see them clairvoyantly. Some

---

[24]**sídh,** also spelled síthe, in Irish folklore, a hill or mound under which fairies live.

Hélèné Fulton

Witches say their Craft (Witchcraft) was passed down from fairies..."
> (Rosemary Ellen Guiley, The Encyclopaedia of Witches and Witchcraft, p. 117)

Fairies come from the underground of hell. "Fairies are generally believed to live as a nation in an underground location..."
> (Harpers' Encyclopedia of Mystical & Paranormal Experience, p. 198)

Fairy tales throughout history have included accounts of evil creatures and Curses and evil spells.

Fairies are a classification of demons that chose to appear as gods and goddesses of pagan times, and more recently as cute little winged creatures or the mischievous "little people" who were once believed to live in hills and wooded areas of Tirna nog, Tirna Nog, according to legend, is the land of eternal youth.

There was an era in Pagan cultures when fairies were revered, and actually worshipped as gods and goddesses. Spirits who appeared to sailors of yore as half woman and half fish were fairies known as mermaids. In some parts of the world, even today, mermaids are worshipped as goddesses. In Africa, a religious sect known as MamiWata worships and makes sacrifices to the goddess of the sea.

In addition to fairies already mentioned, there are kelpies, sylphs, nymphs, elves, silkies, undines, sidhe, nixies, darring, fir, wood fairies, rock fairies, fairies that live underground, fairies of the points of the pentegram: Earth (minerals, metals, elements), Wind (air, gasses), Fire (heat), Rain (water, fluids), and Spirit ("ghosts," apparitions), Fairies of the Mist, and Fairies of the Dew. Depending upon the country, there can be many names for the same fairies. The goddess Rhiannon is the Fairy Queen, goddess of earth and fertility.

But regardless of what these spirits call themselves or how they choose to appear, they are demonic. They're a subgroup of the fallen angels spoken of in Revelation: the ones who were kicked out of Heaven along with Satan when there was war in Heaven. You won't find them called fairies in the Bible. They are found in pagan religions, witchcraft, and folklore, but the fact remains they are very real in the spirit realm.

People worship other gods and give fruits and vegetables as sacrifices. This is strictly forbidden as per Gods Word the Bible.

The Ten Commandments
20 And God spoke all these words, saying:
² "I *am* the L ORD your God, who brought you out of the land of Egypt, out of the house of bondage.

³ **"You shall have no other gods before Me.**
⁴ **"You shall not make for yourself a carved image—any likeness** *of anything* **that** *is* **in heaven above, or that** *is* **in the earth beneath, or that** *is* **in the water under the earth;** ⁵ **you shall not bow down to them nor serve them.** For I, the L ORD your God, *am* a jealous God, visiting the **iniquity of the fathers upon the children to the third and fourth** *generations* **of those who hate Me**, ⁶ but showing mercy to thousands, to those who love Me and keep My commandments.
⁷ "You shall not take the name of the L ORD your God in vain, for the L ORD will not hold *him* guiltless who takes His name in vain.

Hélèné Fulton

⁸ "Remember the Sabbath day, to keep it holy. ⁹ Six days you shall labor and do all your work, ¹⁰ but the seventh day *is* the Sabbath of the LORD your God. *In it* you shall do no work: you, nor your son, nor your daughter, nor your male servant, nor your female servant, nor your cattle, nor your stranger who *is* within your gates. ¹¹ For *in* six days the LORD made the heavens and the earth, the sea, and all that *is* in them, and rested the seventh day. Therefore the LORD blessed the Sabbath day and hallowed it.

¹² "Honor your father and your mother, that your days may be long upon the land which the LORD your God is giving you.

¹³ "You shall not murder.

¹⁴ "You shall not commit adultery.

¹⁵ "You shall not steal.

¹⁶ "You shall not bear false witness against your neighbor.

¹⁷ "You shall not covet your neighbor's house; you shall not covet your neighbor's wife, nor his male servant, nor his female servant, nor his ox, nor his donkey, nor anything that *is* your neighbor's."

Exodus 20

If you serve other gods you do not love God, then you hate God. If you celebrate pagan traditions you are serving pagan gods.

¹⁵ "If you love Me, keep My commandments.

John 14:15

Given the fact that sins of the parents are passed on to their children, even to the third and fourth generation, this will have a great effect on your family and children and their children's health, work, relationships etc. See Exodus 20:4 above.

I have worked with many victims who brought demonic spirits into their lives through books, stories, movies, video games, or an unwise choice of e-mail address. Be careful what you do and say as it will open you up to Satan's attacks.

Whether they take the form of tiny winged creatures, gnomes, leprechauns, or mermaids etc., these are all demonic spirits. Whether it's worship of them, pictures on clothing, toys, jewellery, movies, video games or stories about them, anything on any level having to do with any form of the occult or any form of pagan religion invites demonic spirits into our lives.

Whether you think it's ridiculous or not (and many of you do), the fact that these spirits have the ability and the right to attack the health, finances, and relationships of those unwise enough to have anything to do with them, is reason enough to steer clear of them.

Protection

Types of "Protection" people who are into Religion and the psychic realm frequently use to ward off evil spirits include but are not limited to:

St. Christopher – Crucifix and Rosary

Any item used for protection from demonic forces or from a religion that does not follow the Doctrine of Christ is of the occult, even if it's a crucifix or other religious item such as a St. Christopher medal.

A lady who had a stroke and whose entire right side was lame came to me for help during 2011. I asked the lady if she is a Christian and she said yes she is. I did not know this and during the deliverance God told me to ask her what is around her neck. It was a Catholic rosary.

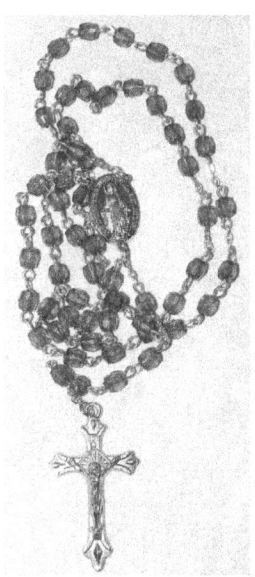

We removed the Rosary from her neck and prayed for her and she was healed. You are not allowed to pray to the Virgin Mary. You are only allowed to pray to Father God through Jesus Christ.

[6] Jesus said to him, "I am the way, the truth, and the life. No one comes to the Father except through Me.

John 14:6

The same goes for the Catholic crucifix

When I told this to a harassment victim I worked with and advised her to dispose of the crucifix she'd been using for protection, demonic spirits manifested by surrounding the crucifix with an electrical charge so she couldn't pick it up. When the spirits causing the electric charge were cast away, the woman was able to pick the crucifix up and dispose of it.
Stacie Spielman

Dream Catchers

In some Native American cultures, a dream catcher (or dream catcher; Lakota: iháŋblagmunka, Ojibwe: asabikeshiinh, the inanimate form of the word for "spider" or Ojibwe: bawaajigenagwaagan meaning "dream snare" is a handmade object based on a willow hoop, on which is woven a loose net or web. The dreamcatcher is then decorated with sacred items such as feathers and beads.

Dream catchers originated with the Ojibwe people and were later adopted by some neighbouring nations through intermarriage and trade. It wasn't until the Pan-Indian Movement of the 1960s and 1970s, that they were adopted by Native Americans of a number of different nations. Some consider the dream catcher a symbol of unity among the various Indian Nations, and a general symbol of identification with Native American or First Nations cultures. However, many other Native Americans have come to see dream catchers as overcommercialized, offensively misappropriated and misused by non-Natives.

The Ojibwe people have an ancient legend about the origin of the dream catcher. Storytellers speak of the Spider Woman, known as Asibikaashi; she took care of the children and the people on the land. Eventually, the Ojibwe Nation spread to the corners of North America and it became difficult for Asibikaashi to reach all the children. So the mothers and grandmothers would weave magical webs for the children, using willow hoops and sinew, or cordage made from plants. The dream catchers would filter out all bad dreams and only allow good thoughts to enter their mind. Once the sun rises, all bad dreams were said to disappear. American ethnographer Frances Densmore writes in her book Chippewa Customs (1929, republished 1979, pg. 113):

Even infants were provided with protective charms. Examples of these are the "spiderwebs" hung on the hoop of a cradle board. These articles consisted of wooden hoops about 3½ inches in diameter filled with an imitation of a spider's web made of fine yarn, usually dyed red. In old times this netting was made of nettle fiber. Two spider webs were usually hung on the hoop, and it was said that they "caught any harm that might be in the air as a spider's web catches and holds whatever comes in contact with it."

Traditionally, the Ojibwe construct dream catchers by tying sinew strands in a web around a small round or tear-shaped frame of willow (in a way roughly similar to their method for making snow shoe webbing). The resulting "dream-catcher", hung above the bed, is used as a charm to protect sleeping people, usually children, from nightmares.

Witchcraft in the Church

The Ojibwe believe that a dream catcher changes a person's dreams. According to Konrad J. Kaweczynski, "Only good dreams would be allowed to filter through… Bad dreams would stay in the net, disappearing with the light of day." Good dreams would pass through and slide down the feathers to the sleeper.

Another explanation of Lakota origin, "Nightmares pass through the holes and out of the window. The good dreams are trapped in the web, and then slide down the feathers to the sleeping person."
                         From Wikipedia, the free encyclopedia

Many children hang this as a decoration in their bedrooms. Remove and burn it immediately as you are inviting demons into your home.

Garlic

Garlic hung in the doorway is said to repel evil spirits and negative energy. This is nothing more than witchcraft.

Holy Water

I have found an enormous number of churches buying "Holy water" from a "Prophet" in Nigeria. I have also helped a large number of people to get out of bondage and demonic oppression and they all used this water. If this water was indeed blessed and holy by God or a true servant of the Lord, do you think that it would have opened these people up for evil spirits. Definitely NOT!

Salt

Some preachers will advise people to sprinkle salt across their threshold and around their house or place of business to ward off evil spirits. Salt attracts them!

Crystals

During April 2013, I've visited some of my spiritual children and at the one spiritual daughter's house; I saw a pentagram over the house in the spiritual world. I took it to the Lord and asked what the opening is for this. She had candles and two crystal pyramids in her house that opened them up for demonic attack.

Smudging

A smudge stick is a bundle of dried herbs, usually bound with string in a small bundle and dried. The herbs are later burned as part of a ritual or ceremony. Plants that are often used include sage and cedar.

The English term "smudge stick" is usually found in use among non-Indigenous people who believe they are practicing appropriated North American Native spiritual traditions. But the herbs used in commercial "smudge sticks", and the rituals performed with them by non-Natives, are rarely the actual materials or rituals used by traditional Native Americans. Using scent and scented smoke in religious rites is an element common to many religions and cultures, but the details and spiritual meanings vary with the specific cultures and ceremonies.

From Wikipedia, the free encyclopedia

To smudge will definitely invite some more demons to your house.

Virgin Mary

Mary was a righteous women and worthy to be chosen to give birth to Jesus Christ. The Bible does NOT say that we should pray to Mary for healing or miracles or even to answer our prayers. We are only allowed to pray to God the Father through Jesus Christ the Son.

The only true protections are the Blood of Jesus Christ and the full armour of God as per Ephesians 6:12 down and the fire of the Holy Spirit.

You may also request from God to give His angels a command to form an army around your house and over your house if you are being attack by witchcraft. Remember you cannot command God's angels, you can only ask God to do this if it is His will.

Hélèné Fulton

Chapter 17: Getting back in line with God

In you have said the salvation prayer before reading this book and you have backslide into the world and the things of the world, then the sermon below by Dr. Rice is for you.

If you have given your heart to Jesus through this book and if you have made Jesus Lord and Savior of your life then I suggest you read my book Only a Born Again will make it into Heaven. Are you ready?

This book will be your next best book after your Bible as it has teachings on what to do after you become born again. It will teach you how to get that personal relationship with God that you've been longing for. It is also a book to help the 5 Fold Ministry to equip the saints.

How to Get Back to Full Fellowship with God
By Dr. John R. Rice

If you are a backslider, then I have good news for you. The simplest and shortest part of this sermon is how to get back to God. Simply turn to God in your heart, confess your sin and backsliding, and He will receive you with open arms and forgive you of all your sins, failures and mistakes.

In 1 John 1:9 is this sweet verse for Christians, "If we confess our sins, he is faithful and just to forgive us our sins, and to cleanse us from all unrighteousness." Isn't that simple? We simply confess our sins honestly, then God is faithful and just to forgive us and cleanse us.

Notice the terms "faithful" and "just." What a strange saying about God! Why, that would seem as if God *owed* it to us to forgive us and cleanse us when we, His wayward children, confess our sin! A man is faithful when he keeps his promises, when he does his duty. Yes, and that is what God is. God is faithful and just to forgive us, when we confess our sin, our backsliding, *because that is within God's bargain!* The keeping. the forgiving, the cleansing day by day is all a part of God's covenant with us when we were saved. All that was purchased for us on Calvary and is promised to every child of God, and so God simply keeps His promise faithfully. Every time we confess our sins, our backslidings, He quickly forgives them and cleanses us from them.

As a young preacher, I preached on the prodigal son. I pictured the long, hard way home. How tired the poor fellow was! How his feet hurt as he stumbled along the rocky road without any shoes! Would he ever get home? And would the father receive him or send him away with scorn? I had that poor, prodigal boy plodding a long, painful way back to the father's house.

Then one day I discovered that I had made that up out of whole cloth. It was not even hinted in that wonderful story as Jesus told it in Luke 15:11-32. In one moment the boy is saying, "I will arise and go to my father." And the very same verse that tells us that the boy "arose, and came to his father," we are told that "when he was yet a great way off, his father saw him, and had compassion, and ran, and fell on his neck and kissed him."

What a lesson for anybody who wants to come to God! Whether for a lost sinner who wants salvation, or a backslider who wants his blessing renewed and his joy restored, it is only one step to the Father's house! Oh, believe me, if you honestly in your heart confess your sin to God, He will forgive you and cleanse you in a moment!

Be sure that you do not excuse your sin. Be sure that you do not make an alibi for it and cover it over. Any honest confession will mean you have a penitent heart that turns from your sin with shame.

And if you feel like weeping, you may weep. I suppose the prodigal boy wept when he came home. I know that when I was a backslider and seemed a long way from God, I wept as I came back to confess my failures and my sins. But remember this: whether there is weeping or no weeping, God wants honest heart-confession of your sin. And when you have confessed your backsliding, your coldness, your lack of joy, then you ought to believe that God has forgiven it as He promised, and that He has cleansed it.

I think it would help you if you would get on your knees and read the fifty-first Psalm and let that divinely inspired prayer be the heart-cry of your own soul. It is the prayer of David, a backslider, and you might let it be your own, too. But remember this: All you need do is to make an honest heart-confession of your sin to the Father and believe that He forgives you as He promised, and that He cleanses you from all your sins. And then you will have sweet fellowship with the Father.

My six daughters are all different. Each one has her own peculiar temptations. One is better about one thing, another is better about another thing. But one of these girls I have never been able to whip very much. For just as certain as she was caught in some sin, some disobedience, she would run and throw her arms around me, and weeping, say, "O Daddy, I'm sorry! I'm so sorry! Forgive me, Daddy!"

Witchcraft in the Church

And so, if the prodigal son has already returned, why should the father send the sheriff and bloodhounds after him? And if the poor backslider is sorry for his sins and is willing to confess them to God, should God lay on the lash of chastisement?

So, backslider, come back today to God with your hungry heart and find peace and forgiveness.

There is a life of victory and joy for every Christian, and you may have it. Since you are still a sinner, you will find that you will need daily to commit your sins to God. First John 1:7 says, "But if we walk in the light, as he is in the light, we have fellowship one with another, and the blood of Jesus Christ his

Son cleanseth us from all sin." You may walk in the light every day. When a sin appears, confess it quickly to God, ask Him to forgive it, and He does then and there. And so every day you may live in the smile of God's presence, in a conscious communion of His blessed Spirit. You need not wait to fall into outbroken sin and shame but can have rich blessing and victory every day.

Perhaps some backslider who reads this today is ready to come back to God. It would comfort my heart, and I believe would make the matter more definite and clear and joyful in your own, if you would write it down and say so. Suppose you write me the following letter, or one similar to it, and send it to me, if you today, dear backslidden Christian, will come back to the Father's house.

References

Bible Knowledge – A special thanks to Michael Bradley for helping me.

Demon Busters
demonbusters.com

End time ministry
http://www.yhwh-glory-end-time-ministry.com/index.php?p=1_15_Cursed-Objects

Bible Truth
http://bible-truths.com/yoked.htm

Stacie Spielman
http://www.staciespielman.com

Dial-the-Truth Ministries, Dr. Terry Watkins, Th.D.
http://www.av1611.org/crock/pod_sym.html

Jesus is Savior dot com

Wikipedia, the free encyclopedia

Exposing Satanism.org

Dr. Peter Hammond
Frontline Fellowship
http://www.frontline.org.za/index.php?option=com_content&view=article&id=998:body-piercing-a-return-to-paganism&catid=16:political-social-issues-cat&Itemid=201

http://www.greatbiblestudy.com

www.ingramcontent.com/pod-product-compliance
Lightning Source LLC
Chambersburg PA
CBHW080423230426
43662CB00015B/2201